BONUS ONLINE CONTENT

Entrepreneur
MAGAZINE'S

ULTIMATE

GUIDE TO

twitter

FOR BUSINESS

- Generate quality leads using only 140 characters
- Instantly connect with **300 million customers in 10 minutes**
- Discover 10 Twitter tools that can be applied now

TED PRODROMOU

EP
Entrepreneur
PRESS®

Entrepreneur Press, Publisher
Cover Design: Andrew Welyczko
Production and Composition: Eliot House Productions

This publication is designed to provide accurate and authoritative information in regard to the
subject matter covered. It is sold with the understanding that the publisher is not engaged in
rendering legal, accounting or other professional services. If legal advice or other expert assistance is
required, the services of a competent professional person should be sought.

Library of Congress Cataloging-in-Publication Data
Prodromou, Ted.
       Ultimate guide to Twitter for business: generate quality leads using 140 characters, instantly
connect with 300 million customers in 10 minutes, discover 10 Twitter tools that can be applied
now / by Ted Prodromou.
       p.   cm.
       ISBN-13: 978-1-59918-449-4 (alk. paper)
       ISBN-10: 1-59918-449-4 (alk. paper)
       1. Internet marketing. 2. Twitter. I. Title.
HF5415.1265.P76 2013
658.8'72—dc23   2012032843

Printed in the United States of America

17 16 15   10 9 8 7 6 5 4 3 2

To my father, Ted, who taught me so much about life. One of his favorite sayings near the end of his life was "When you go to the dance you need to dance," which to me meant that life was about showing up and giving it everything you have. He used to bring me to work with him every summer morning at 7 A.M. so I could help him get our restaurant ready for the day. We used to make everything from scratch every day including the bread, salad dressings, and even the chocolate syrup. I didn't appreciate what he did for me at the time but today I'm so grateful he taught me his work ethic of working hard and doing the very best you can.

Thank you, Dad, and I miss you!

Contents

Acknowledgments

In the summer of 2008 I attended one of Perry Marshall's infamous 4-Man Intensive Workshops at his home in Chicago. It's Perry and just four people brainstorming for two full days. Each person gets an entire half-day of consulting and advice to grow their business. It was an amazing two days for me because I learned as much listening to the advice Perry was giving the other attendees as I did from my half-day session.

Perry's a fabulous teacher, mentor, and business coach, and I've learned so much from him over the past eight years. Little did I know that purchasing his $47 *Definitive Guide to Google AdWords* would change my life forever. Over the years I attended his AdWords Bootcamp twice, which is a 16-week intensive AdWords and marketing course. I also purchased many of his other products and training over the years, but I didn't think Perry knew me from Adam. When I arrived at his house for the Four-Man Intensive, he welcomed me with open arms and he actually knew who I was!

Perry's advice to me in 2008 was to write a book about Twitter because there were no books about Twitter at the time. He was going to introduce me to his publisher and he was sure they would want me to write the book. At the time I didn't think there was enough to write about Twitter to fill an entire book, so I never took action. Big mistake, because about six months later books about Twitter started appearing on Amazon.

Perry taught me so much more than Google AdWords. He taught me about marketing, lead generation, and business building. When the economy turned in 2008 and my business slowed significantly, I was able to find a job as an Online Marketing/ Search Engine Optimization Analyst for a growing software company because of what Perry taught me.

To most people that would be enough, but there's more! About a year ago Perry asked me if I wanted to co-author a book about Twitter. Yes, the same book I should have written four years ago! Of course I was interested because Perry was the author of the best selling Adwords book, so I said yes. For one reason or another, Perry decided he wasn't able to co-author the book, so here we are today. I wrote the entire book myself.

Thank you, Perry, for everything you've done for me and my family. You gave me the knowledge I needed and you inspired me to take the action necessary to change my life for the better. Thank you, Perry!

Foreword
by Susan RoAne

Congratulations! The fact that you have this book in your hand is the first step to building your place in the Twitterverse.

Living in San Francisco and reading our *San Francisco Chronicle's* business section brought Twitter to my attention in 2006. Although I made mention of it in my book *How to Work a Room*, it wasn't until June 2008 that I clearly saw this interesting and different site as a place I wanted to explore. I dipped my Twitter toe in the water.

It was fascinating!

I followed people who I found knowledgeable, interesting, really smart, and fun.

People followed me (although I have no clue how they knew me) and so I followed them back. (Thank you, @ChristianFea and @BalletRusse). I followed those whom they ReTweeted (RT'd), who wrote smart Tweets and included informative URLs. For me, @twitter is higher education in those subjects that didn't exist when most of us were in school.

I soon realized I needed to learn more about this Twitter world: the ins and outs, dos and don'ts, the etiquette, how to build a following, and what to offer in my Tweets.

And talk about timing! An invite to our local Marin SofTECH organization appeared in my inbox. The program was "Twitter: How to

Be Effective," and the guest expert speaker was none other than Ted Prodromou, the author of this book.

Lucky for me, Ted has been a source of support, wise tips and ideas, and encouragement. I learned so much that I was asked to deliver a program to my speaking colleagues on "Twitter as a Speaking Business Tool." Now Ted will be the same coach/mentor/advisor for you. Ted and this book will dramatically cut your Twitter learning curve.

The book is organized in a logical progression and is a complete and thorough how-to guideline to the world of Tweeting from the beginning entry to building your brand. It's everything you need to know and would want to ask.

I sure wish I had it in hand when I first signed on four years ago.

—Susan RoAne, keynote speaker and author of
How to Work a Room and *Face to Face: How to Reclaim the*
Personal Touch in a Digital World

My Twitter Story: Making Friends

Huh?

"Making friends" was my first Tweet on December 5, 2007, at 12:46 PM. What a lame first Tweet! Figure P–1 shows my exciting first Tweet!

Ted Prodromou @tedprodromou
making friends

12:46 PM - 5 Dec 07 via web · Details

← Reply   🗑 Delete   ★ Favorite

FIGURE P–1. My First Tweet. How Embarrassing!

I don't actually remember Tweeting "making friends" and I have no idea why I Tweeted that. That isn't something I would say to anyone in a conversation, but maybe I was at a holiday lunch and had a few too many eggnogs!

Twitter started in March 2006 and was called Twttr at the time. I signed up because I was starting to see more and more articles about Twttr online. I'm usually an early adopter when it comes to new technology and online communities, so I created my account. I remember the Twitter handle *tedprodromou* wasn't available for some reason, which surprised me because my name is pretty unique. I decided to go with *l3fty*, which was a nickname I used to use when signing up for online accounts because I am left-handed. Eventually I changed *l3fty* to *ted_prodromou* and grabbed *tedprodromou* when it became available a few years later.

When I first joined Twitter, like most people, I didn't know what to say. Twitter used to prompt you with the question "What are you doing?" These prompts are supposed to inspire you to share what you're doing. The Tweets that appeared from the prompt, "What are you doing?" were not very compelling. The initial Tweets I used to see were something like:

I'm going grocery shopping

Off to the gym

Standing in line at Starbucks

Lunching with friends at Applebees

You get the idea. The Tweets were boring as hell, so I didn't become an instant Twitter fan. In fact, I didn't think Twitter would survive because it was so boring. I checked out the Who to Follow recommendations on my Twitter page and started following some people who looked interesting. There weren't many people on Twitter at the time, so the list was pretty limited. I followed some people who had similar interests as mine. I followed some people interested in technology, hiking, and skiing.

The Tweets didn't get any better.

I have the worst headache

I need another cup of coffee!

Where is the nearest Starbucks?

My cramps are so bad today

I hate it when (fill in the blank)

I'm waiting for my Dominos delivery. Mmmmmmm

Twitter was becoming an online bitchfest for many of the early users. I guess people weren't used to being limited to 140 characters, so their Tweets were not very creative at first. It is hard to be expressive in just a few words when you aren't used to being limited to short messages. I still have that problem today when I'm thinking of something to say in my Tweets. You want to be clever and interesting when you Tweet, and your creativity seems to disappear when you think of that 140-character limit. Total mind block occurs. It really makes you appreciate the people on Twitter who do it well.

I continued to experiment and monitor Twitter as the community grew. I primarily used Twitter to promote my blog posts and to see how others were using Twitter. I followed more and more people so I could watch them and see if they were successful with Twitter. I had no idea what being successful at Twitter meant at the time because it was still evolving and it was like a blank slate with no rules. Millions of people were joining Twitter to see what the buzz was about but nobody really understood what to do because there were no rules or guidelines. In fact, most people who signed up for Twitter stopped using it after the first month because they didn't see any value in it. Considering most Tweets were complaints or people sharing their inner voice with us (way too much information in most cases!), I can see why people quit using Twitter after a month or so.

The next Twitter trend began when people started Tweeting pictures of their food. It seemed like some people were Tweeting pictures of everything they ate. I have to admit I did it a few times but not for long. It was interesting for a very short time, and thank God that trend faded away pretty quickly.

Of course when one trend fades away, another takes its place. That would be the introduction of the apps like Foursquare, where you check in everywhere you go. You could follow someone all over the world and know what restaurants they hang out at, what hotels they like, and more information than you would ever want to know about that person by seeing their Foursquare check-ins. If you follow @stevewozniak, you will see where he is at all times. He uses Foursquare to check in everywhere he goes, even when he returns to his home. Personally, I think it's a bad idea to let people know when you are out of town because they know your house is unattended, but Steve doesn't seem to care. I never got into the "check-in" thing and never wanted to be the mayor of any local businesses.

For some reason, I stuck with Twitter even though it wasn't providing much value to me. I guess I found it entertaining in a strange way. I would log in every day to see what was happening in the Twitterverse and read those boring Tweets, hoping the conversations would get more entertaining or educational. Many Tweeters never evolved past that "sharing my deep inner thoughts" stage, so I started unfollowing those people. I didn't care if they were craving another cup of coffee or had the stomach flu. Once I started filtering out the whiners and complainers, I started seeing some value from the people I was following.

Over time, people learned how to use Twitter to share valuable information or tips. Companies began using Twitter to give away discount coupons for their products and services. Twitter contests started popping up and Tweetups, in-person get-togethers or networking events promoted exclusively on Twitter, started forming. Tweetups are usually impromptu events held at local restaurants or bars for people with like interests. My first Tweetup was in 2008 when Peter Shankman (@petershankman) was coming to San Francisco on a business trip. Someone organized a Tweetup a couple of days before he arrived and we all met at a popular San Francisco restaurant for happy hour and appetizers. About 100 people showed up for the last-minute event, and we all got to meet Peter and drink a few beers with him. I met a lot of San Francisco people who were interested in the new phenomenon called social media and worked in the tech industry. I still hang out with some of the people I met at that event and will never forget my first Tweetup.

A funny thing happened after following people on Twitter for a while. I realized the people I was following were becoming my virtual friends. I never met these people and never interacted with most of them, but I knew a lot about them from reading their Tweets. I knew what kind of food they liked, what restaurants they ate at, where they vacationed and what they liked and disliked. I would look forward to reading about what projects they're working on, what they do for fun, and whom they hang out with. It's like I'd known them all my life even though we never met in person or even spoke on the phone. It sounds creepy, but I guess it's no different than following the lives of celebrities by reading the tabloids or watching *TMZ*. People who Tweet a lot are becoming online celebrities with huge followings. A very easy way for you to become a thought leader in your industry is Tweeting on a regular basis and building a large following.

You can learn a lot about a person by reading their past and current Tweets. People can go to your Twitter page and read your previous Tweets, so be careful what you Tweet! In the past, Twitter only published the Tweets from the previous week, but they've expanded their capacity and now your homepage displays a longer history of Tweets. I don't know the exact number of Tweets they save, and they're not telling, but it looks like you can go back a long way. I checked my previous Tweets and the history goes back to my very first Tweet. If you Tweet constantly and have more than 20,000 Tweets, as some people do, I'm not sure how many they display.

As you see, I'm not a huge Tweeter and I don't have a million followers. I tend to keep a low profile on Twitter personally because of my job. I do most of my Tweeting from our corporate Twitter accounts and focus my efforts there. I do use Twitter as a search engine to research our competitors and the computer software industry.

I read an article online (MediaBistro.com) recently that talked about a study of Twitter users. I don't remember exactly where I read the article because I scan my Google Reader account daily and read a ton of articles. The study said women tend to Tweet more personal information and Tweet more often than guys. Men use Twitter more for research and to follow leaders in their industry. Sounds like real life, doesn't it? Women like to express their feelings and talk more than men do!

I use Twitter every day, primarily to monitor our brand, the computer software industry, and our competitors. I do Tweet from my personal account to share relevant articles with my followers. I have my Twitter account connected to my LinkedIn account so my Tweets appear in my LinkedIn status updates. I'll show you how to connect your Twitter account to your blog and other social media accounts later in this book.

So that's my Twitter story. I've been on Twitter for a long time and I've grown to really enjoy my Twitter family and friends. I'll admit there were times I lost interest on and off, but these days I log in every day and Tweet as often as I feel is appropriate. I don't Tweet just to Tweet. I only Tweet when I have something interesting to say or some great information to share. Our time is precious and I don't want to waste my followers' time by Tweeting what I'm eating for lunch or how I feel that day. Follow me at @tedprodromou and join my Twitter family.

Also visit www.tedprodromou.com/twitter to see bonus videos that show you step by step how to get started with Twitter if you are a beginner and advanced Twitter techniques that will set you apart from your competition.

Why Twitter?

Twitter has taken the internet by storm. It's not growing as fast as Facebook, but Twitter has become a powerful news and marketing channel. More often than not, eyewitnesses are breaking news around the world on Twitter before international media outlets can arrive at the scene to report it.

I believe Twitter isn't as popular as Facebook or other social media websites because most people don't get Twitter. They don't understand the power of short, timely messages that catch our attention like powerful media headlines or interesting email subject lines. Twitter is a great tool to interrupt someone's thought process and grab their attention. Whether you are a Twitter fan or not, you can't ignore the fact that it has become an integral part of our lives. You see Twitter hashtags everywhere. You see them in all major advertising campaigns, whether in print, billboards, online, and in TV ads. Twitter is here to stay!

In this book, you will learn Twitter's history and how Twitter is changing our social behavior. Who would have imagined that giving someone the ability to send 140-character messages would help organize revolutions and protests in countries around the world? We'll explore how Twitter is being used to report breaking news related to politics and sports around the world in real time. We'll also explore how many celebrities are using Twitter to keep in touch with their fans while earning money doing promoted Tweets.

In Chapter 2, you'll learn the basics of Twitter, including the Twitter commands and lingo. If you don't know what to say on Twitter, I'll help you get over your shyness so you can engage others in Twitter conversations. Next, I'll help you customize your Twitter profile so you can attract the right followers and appear in Twitter searches. This will help you get the word out about your company so you can get free publicity.

You'll also learn how to create a comprehensive Twitter strategy for you and your company. Who should you follow? How many people should you follow? How often should you Tweet? Once you create your Twitter strategy, you'll know exactly how to use Twitter to grow your business.

After you create your Twitter strategy, I'll teach you some advanced Twitter techniques. Once you learn them, you'll be head and shoulders above your competition; most Twitter users only use the basic Twitter functions. You'll know how to generate targeted leads, create fun Twitter contests to grow your followers, drive traffic to your website or blog, and create viral Tweets that will publicize your brand.

In Chapter 8, I'll show you the latest and greatest Twitter tools that will enhance your Twitter experience. You'll be able to monitor your competition, grow your follower list, promote your products and services, and drive traffic to your blog and website 24/7.

In Chapter 9, I'll share some Twitter success stories with you. These are people just like you and me who have used Twitter to grow their businesses. These aren't Twitter power users like Chris Brogan and Ashton Kutcher. These are small-business owners who have successfully used Twitter to promote and grow their businesses.

Of course, no Twitter book would be complete without a list of Twitter power users. This is a list of the people I follow to learn the latest Twitter techniques and to see how they used Twitter to become thought leaders in their industries.

Let's get started by taking a look at some facts about Twitter and how fast it's growing.

CONNECTING WITH OTHERS

You have friends on Facebook and connections on LinkedIn. On Twitter you have followers, who are people who "subscribe" to your updates. Every time you Tweet, it shows up on your followers' timelines. When you become someone's follower, you'll see all of their Tweets on your timeline.

One huge difference between Facebook, LinkedIn, and Twitter is that on Twitter you don't have to ask permission to follow someone. We all know about the friend requests on Facebook and the connection requests on LinkedIn. You can approve, deny, or ignore connection requests from others. With Twitter, anyone can follow you and you can follow anyone and see their Tweets, as long as they haven't set their profile to *Protect my Tweets.*

For some reason I have a strange vision when I think of Twitter. I'm not sure if you remember the old TV commercials for Ricola cough drops. The commercial is set in the Swiss Alps and there's a guy standing on top of a mountain peak singing "Riiicooolaaa" into the beautiful valleys below. While he's passionately singing "Riiicooolaaa" from this mountaintop, how does he know if anyone is listening? Does he care if anyone is listening? Probably not. He's all alone, miles from anyone, but he still shares his message with the world.

I think of Twitter in the same way. Everyone is Tweeting messages into the Twitterverse, but is anyone listening? If you don't have any followers, probably not many are seeing your message, but if you add a popular hashtag to the Tweet, millions may see your message. People are sharing their inner thoughts and passions on Twitter, like the guy standing on the mountaintop singing "Riiicooolaaa."

When you first join Twitter, it feels like you are speaking to yourself when you Tweet because you don't get a response most of the time. The silence can be deafening. As you get better at Tweeting and using hashtags, you start receiving responses to your Tweets, which is really cool.

I remember the first response I received on Twitter. I think it was my third or fourth Tweet and I Tweeted about the P90X video workout program that I just started doing. I Tweeted something like "P90X day 1—what a killer workout" and added #P90X at the end of my Tweet. I received an immediate response from someone else who was further along in the workouts. She praised me for starting the P90X program, which is very intense, and encouraged me to keep it up.

I was so excited that I got a response, I started monitoring the #P90X hashtag, which helped support me through the program. That was my first Twitter conversation and it was so cool!

TWITTER FACTS

Officially, Twitter announced in 2011 that it has 100 million active users. An active Twitter user is a member who logs in at least once a month. Twitter has been growing rapidly since September 2011, so the number of active users is estimated to be 150 million according to many social media experts. Figure 1–1 on page 4 shows the growth of active Twitter users. Twitter doesn't share their exact usage data on a regular basis, so it's hard to confirm these numbers, but the estimates are usually in the ballpark.

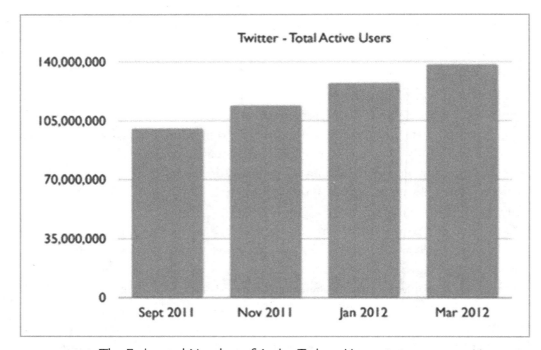

FIGURE 1–1. The Estimated Number of Active Twitter Users. *Source*: www.twopblog.com

How many total users does Twitter have? In April 2011, Katie Stanton, Twitter's vice president of international strategy, announced that the platform had 200 million registered accounts. In May 2011, the total registered accounts were estimated to be 300 million according to independent Twitter account tracker Twopcharts. In August 2011, this figure had risen to 362 million, and it passed 400 million a couple of months later, according to the Twopcharts estimates. In February 2012, Twopcharts estimated Twitter surpassed the 500,000-registered-users milestone. Figure 1–2 on page 5 shows the estimated number of registered Twitter users. Twitter did announce that they were receiving 400 million unique visitors per month in September 2011, confirming their rapid growth.

The registered number of users can be deceiving because there are many fraudulent accounts, abandoned accounts, and accounts used by bots that create Twitter spam. There is no way to know how many of these accounts exist, but 500,000 is still a pretty impressive number of registered accounts.

Facebook is approaching one billion accounts, and a number of those accounts are fraudulent or abandoned, which is common with all social media platforms. The important number when measuring the success of a social media site is the number of active users who log in at least once a month. Over half of Facebook's members log in *every day,* which is staggering. The fact that Twitter has over 150 million active users and

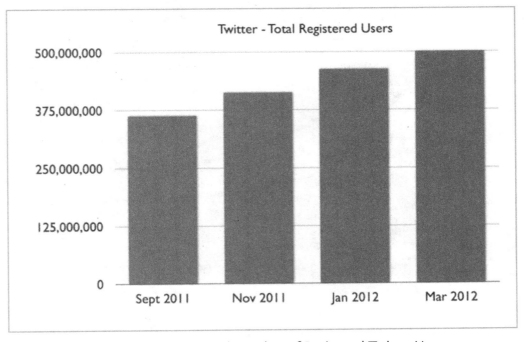

FIGURE 1–2. The Estimated Number of Registered Twitter Users.

Source: www.twopblog.com

is still growing fast is a good sign that Twitter will be a powerful force in our lives for quite a while.

IS TWITTER FOR YOU?

Many people have a love/hate relationship with Twitter. If you take the time to learn Twitter and understand its power, you love it. If you sign up and don't explore the possibilities, you write it off as a waste of time.

One thing you can't ignore is the growth and popularity of Twitter. Yes, it's not as big as Facebook, but most power Twitter users find it infinitely more useful. Twitter is growing at a faster rate than Facebook, as you see in Figure 1–3 on page 6.

This study by eMarketer in March 2012 predicts Twitter will grow faster than Facebook for the next couple of years. Will Twitter ever reach one billion users as Facebook approaches that astronomical number? Probably not, because many people are freaked out by the 140-character limit. They don't believe Twitter can be useful for business. When Google+ launched, many people were excited because they weren't limited to 140 characters, but Google+ doesn't seem to be slowing Twitter's growth at all. People and businesses are still struggling to figure out how to leverage Google+.

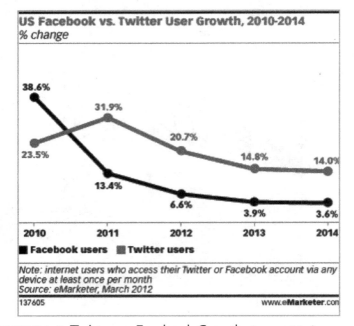

FIGURE 1–3. Twitter vs. Facebook Growth. *Source:* eMarketer.com

There are thousands of success stories from businesses that use Twitter to grow. I'll be sharing some of them later in this book so you can see how powerful Twitter can be when you think out of the box (sorry for that old cliché!). Everywhere you look, you see Twitter hashtags on billboards, magazine ads, newspaper ads, and TV commercials and shows.

Twitter has hit the mainstream and you can't ignore it. Your prospects and customers are on Twitter and they're talking about you. Your competitors are using Twitter to prospect for new customers, to support their current customers, and to build stronger relationships with their current customers. If you don't use Twitter for your business, you are missing out on some significant opportunities.

Twitter has found a niche as the outlet for breaking news. Almost every significant breaking news event is reported on Twitter before it's reported to the major media outlets. This is because eyewitnesses are Tweeting breaking news as it happens before the media outlets can get there to cover the event. You can leverage the popularity of Twitter to get the news out about your business by announcing new products, promotional events, specials, and holding Twitter contests.

Take a look at Figure 1–4 on page 7. The media gets it. Twitter is in the news almost daily for some reason. The continued popularity of Twitter among celebrities is a source of news itself, which effectively guarantees an onslaught of news items. Evolving world events also puts Twitter in the news frequently.

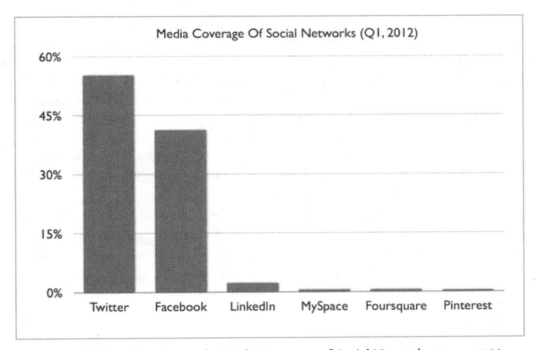

FIGURE 1–4. Twitter Dominates the Media Coverage of Social Networks. *Source*: Highbeam Research (www.highbeam.com)

Maybe you don't feel comfortable Tweeting about your business, or you don't think your prospects or customers are on Twitter. It's OK not to be a frequent Tweeter. You can be a passive Twitter user and just monitor your brand name, your competitors, and some keyword phrases related to your industry. I'm sure you will quickly see the potential value of Twitter when you see how many conversations are happening related to your business or industry. Once you see the value, you can start experimenting with some Tweets to drive people to your blog or website.

The fact is that Twitter is for you and your business, so I invite you to get started today!

SOCIAL IMPACT

When Twitter started in 2006, nobody could have known that it would have such a dramatic impact on our lives. Who would have thought Twitter would play such a significant role in world events like the Egyptian revolution in 2011, the Tunisian protests in 2010–2011, and the Iranian election protests in 2009–2010?

Protesters used thousands of Tweets with specific hashtags to coordinate their activities and provide up-to-the-second updates to their followers. Within minutes, thousands of protestors assembled at targeted locations powering the revolutions. Today, Twitter has become the default communication tool for social movements around the world.

Probably the most surprising social movement occurred in 2008 when Barack Obama used Twitter and social media to engage 18- to 25-year-olds in the United States to win the presidential election. Never before had a presidential candidate used social media to engage an audience, and it turned out to be a brilliant strategic move. Today, every political candidate uses Twitter during their campaigns to reach out to the voters, and very often they use Twitter as their initial media channel to make major announcements.

Twitter has touched virtually every aspect of our lives including celebrities, entertainment, sports, news, business, religion, politics, and even weather reports. Many people use Twitter to keep up with current events and to communicate with friends and co-workers. Private Twitter channels are often used to communicate privately between groups of friends or teams of co-workers in corporations.

Current Events

Every major media outlet now uses Twitter extensively. News anchorpeople and reporters display their Twitter handles below their names when they are on the air. TV and radio stations use Twitter to communicate breaking events to their followers. Many TV stations invite viewers to Tweet pictures of breaking events to them using Instagram or Twitpic. News reporting has become an interactive activity between the viewers and the news reporters, providing up-to-the-second reports complete with pictures.

The Arab Spring

On December 19, 2010, Mohamed Bouazizi set fire to himself in Tunisia in protest after police confiscated the fruit and vegetables he was selling from a street stall. Riots broke out and the event became a Twitter Top Story, attracting thousands of protesters in minutes. People were angry at the mistreatment of Bouazizi and the deterioration of employment in the region. Riots spread through Tunisia over the next few weeks, resulting in Tunisia's President Zine al-Abidine Ben Ali to flee the country.

This was the beginning of a series of Middle Eastern events that became known as the Arab Spring, and Twitter played a vital role in these events, because news is often censored in these countries. Protestors were able to communicate freely and without censorship to coordinate the protests. When the governments tried to block access to Twitter and/or the internet, the protests grew even faster.

On January 1, 2011, a bomb exploded in Egypt, killing 21 people. This bombing set off civil unrest, resulting in the eventual overthrow of Prime Minister Hosni Mubarak on February 11. Protests continued for months as citizens demanded prosecution of Mubarak for his years of human rights violations.

Civil unrest spread to Bahrain, Jordan, Iran, Israel, Kuwait, Lebanon, Libya, Morocco, Oman, Palestine, Saudi Arabia, Syria, and Yemen. Muammar Gaddafi of Libya and Ali Abdullah Saleh of Yemen were also overthrown.

Twitter proved to be a powerful communication tool that let tightly controlled and censored citizens rise up and overthrow their inhumane leaders after years of corruption and abuse. And you thought you couldn't say anything meaningful in 140 characters? Think again!

Sporting Events

Whether you are a New York Yankees fan or a Manchester City FC fan, you will find a strong following of passionate fans on Twitter. Professional and college sports teams have embraced it as a way to engage their fans, and the results have been phenomenal.

I'm a San Francisco Giants baseball fan and I was amazed at the amount of Twitter activity when they won the World Series in 2010. Fans were Tweeting about every pitch, every at bat and every play in the field. After the final out of the game, with the team celebrating like a bunch of kids on the field, my Twitter stream on TweetDeck was jammed. Thousands of Tweets per second throttled the Twitter stream for #SFGiants and it took hours to clear out.

What amazed me the most about following the #SFGiants hashtag is that the chatter doesn't stop after the baseball season ends. There is a steady stream of Tweets every day of the year, even in the winter, when the team is idle. People are passionate about their sports teams and they love to Tweet their thoughts about them constantly. Sports teams are realizing this and are actively Tweeting and engaging fans to keep the buzz going year round. This keeps the fans excited about the team, which can increase ticket sales and the sale of team souvenirs.

Twitter is also very popular with football and basketball teams. The NBA recently announced they are adding the players' Twitter handles to their souvenir jerseys. NBA players love to Tweet their thoughts and often engage with fans on Twitter.

The NFL added new rules a couple of years ago prohibiting players from Tweeting during games. They are also prohibited from Tweeting or updating their social media profiles 90 minutes before a game or until the post-game interviews are concluded. Athletes love to vent on social media and Twitter has become their tool of choice.

Celebrities

Many say Twitter's growth is directly related to celebrities. A few years ago, Ashton Kutcher declared he wanted to be the first Twitter user with a million followers. At the time, nobody had anywhere near a million followers, and they thought it was impossible for someone to have that many. He launched a massive publicity campaign that worked. Once Kutcher hit a million followers, other celebrities jumped on board, including Oprah. Once Oprah embraces something, the world seems to follow.

Not to be outdone, Lady Gaga was the first Twitter user to hit 10 million, then 20 million followers. Today she has over 25 million followers and communicates with them many times a day. She always says "good night" to her fans, which excites them to no end. She genuinely seems to enjoy Tweeting to her followers, but you have to wonder if she's doing it because she really loves them or because she enjoys the $30 million she earns every year for sponsored Tweets. I'd love my fans a lot more if I were earning $30 million a year!

Live Interaction While Watching TV Shows

This is a phenomenon I discovered a few years ago when I was checking out www.Tweetstats.com, which is a site that shows trending topics and popular hashtags. At the time, *American Idol* was on TV and the number of Tweets using their hashtags was pegged off the chart. The rest of the week was a flat line of a few Tweets per day, but the chart spiked dramatically while the show was on the air. I looked at the Tweets and the viewers were Tweeting in real time about every contestant's performance, their hair, their clothing, and how much they loved them. Twitter users were engaged in real-time conversations with each other all over the country. It totally amazed me.

Network TV noticed this, too, and now every TV show displays a Twitter handle in the footer of your TV screen so you can interact with other viewers. Some reality shows even have the host Tweeting live during the show and engaging with the viewers.

The results? In this age of DVRs and on-demand viewing, very few people were watching shows live. They watched them when it was convenient for them or they watched them on the internet through sites like www.hulu.com. Today, more people are watching live TV again so they can engage with other viewers while they watch the show. You will see a spike in Twitter activity for every popular TV show while the show airs. This makes TV executives and advertisers very happy because it means viewers won't be fast forwarding through the commercials.

CONCLUSION

Twitter is affecting our society in ways that nobody ever imagined. Most experts expected Twitter to fade away because of the 140-character limitation, but businesses are constantly finding new ways to leverage the power of Twitter to spread the word about their brand. Twitter is being incorporated into every aspect of our lives and is becoming a common communication channel for business, media, and for personal communication.

In the next chapter, we'll explore the fundamentals of Twitter so you can see how simple it is to use, and we'll get you Tweeting like the experts in no time.

The ABCs of Twitter

You have to walk before you can run, so this is a good place to start. We'll begin by learning the Twitter lingo that you hear on the news. Once you get familiar with the Twitter language, in Chapter 3 I'll teach you about the history of Tweeting and why it's limited to only 140 characters. The short messages and constant chatter on Twitter is the main reason many people don't even attempt to Tweet. They don't know what to say, or they don't think they can say anything meaningful in 140 characters. As you'll see, there's an art to creating meaningful messages in 140 characters and it becomes addicting once you get the hang of it. I'll help you get started Tweeting and get you over the fear of posting your first Tweet. Learning the Twitter lingo will give you courage.

TWITTER LINGO

Like most technology, Twitter has its own language. I'm sure you've heard the terms Tweet and ReTweet, but you probably have no idea what they mean. Let's look at the most common Twitter terms so you'll know what everyone's talking about.

@

The @ sign is used to call out usernames in Tweets. You can say something like: "Hey @tedprodromou!" The @ works differently in Twitter than it does in an email address. When a username is preceded by the @ sign, it becomes a link to a Twitter profile. When you click on that link you will be able to view the person's profile to learn more about them.

@Message

If you want to send a public message to somebody, you start your Tweet with the @ followed by their Twitter name or handle. For example, if you want to send a message to me, you start your Tweet with @tedprodromou followed by the message you want to send me in the Tweet.

In the early days of Twitter there was no way for you to send a message directly to another user. Twitter was a one-way conversation at that point. You could post your status updates or Tweets, but there was no way for people to respond to you. That was frustrating to most users because they wanted to have conversations on Twitter and respond to what people were posting. The only thing people could do when they wanted to respond to something someone else posted, and have that person see it, was start a Tweet with the @ sign and the person's Twitter handle.

Eventually Twitter realized people wanted to hold conversations online, so they incorporated these user-generated features into Twitter. This feature became a key networking tool for Twitter users and greatly enhances Twitter's functionality. @ Messages became known as @mentions or @replies.

DM

All Twitter messages are public by default. That means everyone can see all of your Tweets. If you want to send a personal message directly to someone who's following you on Twitter, you can send them a direct message (DM). This is like sending your friend a text message on their phone, where only they receive it. A direct message in Twitter is also like sending a short email directly to your friend. Only you and your friend know what is contained in that message. Direct messages work exactly the same way.

Discover

The Discover tab on your Twitter page is where you find Stories, Who to Follow, Activity, Find Friends, and Browse Categories.

Fail Whale

In the early days of Twitter it was growing so fast that it often exceeded its capacity. Occasionally there were long periods of time when it wasn't possible to access Twitter.

It got so bad that Twitter created its own logo called "the fail whale," which they would post on the Twitter website when it exceeded capacity. Twitter still has occasional hiccups, but for the most part the system is more reliable than ever.

Favorite

To *Favorite* a Tweet means to mark it as one of your favorites. You Favorite a Tweet by clicking on the star next to the message as shown in Figure 2–1. You can also Favorite via SMS, or text messaging via your phone. People love to see their Tweets Favorited, so do it when you want to show your appreciation to someone for creating a catchy or thought-provoking Tweet.

> **Susan RoAne** @susanroane   12m
> Looking fwd to speaking today to GE's Senior Leaders & the Silicon
> Valley Leadership Group's BBCUE @49ers new facility.
> Collapse ← Reply ⇄ Retweet ★ Favorite

FIGURE 2–1. You Can Easily Reply, ReTweet, or Favorite a Tweet

Follow

To follow someone on Twitter is to subscribe to their Tweets or updates by clicking on the *Follow* button in their profile. The more people you follow, the more Tweets you will see in your Tweet stream, giving you more opportunity to engage others in conversation.

Follower

A follower is another Twitter user who has followed you. The more followers you have, the more popular you are on Twitter. Celebrities often have millions of followers while normal people like you and I can have thousands of followers if they are active on Twitter.

Handle

A user's "Twitter handle" is the username they have selected and the accompanying URL. Your Twitter handle is also referred to as your Twitter name. My Twitter handle is officially http://twitter.com/tedprodromou.

Hashtag

The # symbol, called a *hash* mark and when used to mark keywords or topics in a Tweet it is called a *hashtag*. Its use began organically as Twitter users sought a way to categorize messages. Today, most Tweets contain a # and a keyword so people can easily follow a Twitter conversation involving sometimes thousands of people.

Almost every TV show displays the show's hashtag at the bottom of the screen so viewers can Tweet with each other during the show. It's an amazing phenomenon that has revolutionized TV watching and is actually getting people to watch shows live instead of recording them.

Interactions

Your Twitter Interactions is the timeline in your @ Connect tab that displays all ways other users have interacted with your account, like adding you to a list, sending you a reply, Favoriting one of your Tweets, ReTweeting one of your Tweets. As you see in Figure 2–2, viewing your @ Connect tab is a quick way to see who's engaging with you if you aren't using one of the Twitter tools to monitor your activity.

FIGURE 2–2. You Can View Your Twitter Interactions on the @ Connect Tab

Listed

When someone adds you to a Twitter list, you are considered to be listed. The number of times you are listed appears in the statistics section of your profile.

Lists

Lists are curated groups of other Twitter users. Twitter Lists are like distribution lists in email where you group people together so you can easily communicate with everyone at once. Another benefit of using Twitter Lists is that you can group people you are following by topics so you can quickly see the latest trends or conversations. For example, I created a list called SEO and added the Search Engine Optimization experts I follow on

Twitter. By viewing this list, I can easily see what the top SEO experts are talking about in one organized column in HootSuite or TweetDeck. Twitter Lists are sort of like Groups on Facebook or LinkedIn where you can join in targeted conversations based on specific topics.

Mention

Mentioning another user in your Tweet by including the @ sign followed directly by their username is called a "mention." Another way to Mention someone is to add their username in a Tweet. If someone Tweeted, "Hey @tedprodromou I loved your blog post about Twitter," it would be considered a Mention. If they Tweeted, "Hey tedprodromou," it would also appear as a Mention.

Name

A name can be different from your username and is used to locate you on Twitter. Your name must be 20 characters or less. For example, my name on Twitter is Ted Prodromou, but my username is tedprodromou.

Profile

The Twitter page that displays information about a Twitter user, as well as all the Tweets they have posted from their account, is the profile page. Your profile also includes your bio, which is a 160-character description of you.

Promoted Tweets

These are Tweets that are paid promotions or ads at the top of search results on Twitter. Promoted Tweets are targeted by keywords so they only appear at appropriate times. I'll explain Promoted Tweets in greater detail in Chapter 7, "Advanced Twitter."

Protected/Private Accounts

All Twitter accounts are public by default. You can choose to protect your account so your Tweets will only be seen by approved followers and will not appear in Twitter Search. This is a great way for remote business teams to share information and keep in touch with each other when working together on projects.

Reply

A Reply is a Tweet that is posted in reply to another user's message. A Reply is usually posted by clicking the "reply" button next to their Tweet in your timeline. A Reply always begins with @username. If the @username is not the first word in the Tweet, it is considered a Mention.

RT or ReTweet

When you like someone's Tweet you can forward it to your Twitter followers by ReTweeting it. I like to add comments to my ReTweets to let people know why I'm Tweeting it. This can get tricky if the original Tweet is very long because of the 140-character limit. Sometimes you just have to ReTweet it without a comment. ReTweeting is like forwarding a funny joke someone emailed to you, or sharing a Facebook post you like.

RSS Feed

RSS is commonly known as Really Simple Syndication. RSS is a set of web feed formats used to publish frequently updated works—such as blog entries or news headlines—in a standardized format. RSS automates the process of publishing content on websites and blogs.

Search or Twitter Search

The box in the top right corner of your Twitter homepage is the Twitter Search box. Twitter Search lets you search all public Tweets for keywords, usernames, hashtags, or subjects. Searches can also be performed at http://search.twitter.com. Twitter Search works just like any other search engine but the results are limited to Twitter content.

Short Code

A short code is the five-digit phone number used to send and receive Tweets via text message.

Stories

Stories on Twitter are found in the Discover tab as you see in Figure 2–3 on page 19. Think of Stories as expanded Trends. Stories are the Trends plus the links to the video, images, blogs, and web content mentioned in the Tweet.

Text Commands

Before apps for your smartphones, you had to enter text commands to send your Tweets. Today the text commands are built into the apps so you don't have to worry about them.

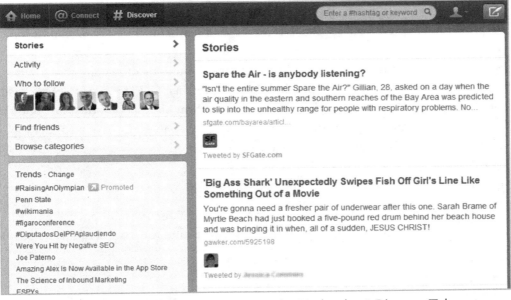

FIGURE 2–3. You Can See Twitter Stories Under the # Discover Tab

Some example text commands are:

- FOLLOW @username
- UNFOLLOW @username
- D [username] + message
- RT [username]

You get the message. Thankfully we now have apps that handle the text commands behind the scenes.

Timeline

Your Timeline is a real time list of Tweets from users you're following on Twitter.

Timestamp

Every Tweet is time stamped, which can be found in gray text directly below any Tweet. The timestamp is also a link to that Tweet's own URL.

Top Tweets

Top Tweets are determined by a Twitter algorithm to be the most popular or resonant on Twitter at any given time. They are usually Tweets by people with the most followers or by people who Tweet often.

Trends

With over 150 million Twitter users Tweeting over 500 million Tweets a day, some topics become more popular than others. When a major earthquake hits Japan or a terrorist bomb explodes in the Middle East, thousands if not millions of people start Tweeting about the event. Usually they will add a hashtag to their Tweets so people can easily follow that topic. The *Trends* list on Twitter is a real-time summary of the most popular topics being Tweeted about at that moment. You can see an example of trending topics in the left column of Figure 2–3 on page 19.

Tweet

A Tweet refers to a single Twitter post or text message. Your Twitter homepage consists of your timeline, which is a history of all your Tweets and the Tweets of all the people you're following.

Tweeter

An account holder on Twitter who posts and reads Tweets is a Tweeter; also known as a Twitterer.

Tweetup

An in-person networking event that is promoted almost exclusively via Twitter is called a Tweetup. Tweetups have become very popular because you can quickly bring together a group of like-minded people who are following each other on Twitter. When you publicize the Tweetup on Twitter, the general public sees the invitation so you can attract new people to your networking groups with little effort.

Unfollow

When you want to stop following another Twitter user, you unfollow them. Their Tweets no longer show up in your home timeline. I often unfollow people if they automate their Tweets and/or do not provide any valuable information.

URL Shortener

URL shorteners are used to turn long URLs into shorter URLs. Shortening your URLs is important because you only have 140 characters available for your Tweets. Some URL shorteners include www.bit.ly, www/TinyURL.com, www.Ow.ly and many others.

Username

Your username is also known as your Twitter handle. Your username must be unique and contain fewer than 15 characters. It is also used to identify you on Twitter for replies and mentions.

Verification

A process whereby a user's Twitter account is stamped to show that a legitimate source is authoring the account's Tweets is a verification. It is sometimes used for accounts that have experienced identity confusion, or to verify a celebrity's real identity for their Twitter account.

Who to Follow

You'll find Who to Follow in the # Discover tab. You will see a few recommendations of accounts the Twitter algorithm thinks you'll find interesting. The recommendations are based on the types of accounts you're already following and who those people follow.

Widget

A widget is a bit of code that can be placed anywhere on the web. Widgets are very common in content management websites like WordPress, Drupal, and Joomla. A widget placed on your website or blog can automatically display your Twitter updates in real time.

CONCLUSION

As you see, Twitter has its own language that is pretty easy to learn. The good news is that most Twitter apps, whether for your desktop computer or your smartphone, do most of the work for you. In the past, when you wanted to send a message to someone you had to type the text commands into the *Compose new Tweet* box on www.twitter.com. Actually Twitter used the phrase "What are you doing?" to prompt your Tweets. They changed that after a couple of years because they discovered it was limiting what people would say in their Tweets. Now they leave the text box open-ended and let you express yourself any way you want to.

Now that you know the Twitter lingo, let's move on to the next chapter where I'll walk step by step through the signup process. Once we create your Twitter account, I'll teach you the basics of Twitter etiquette, and get you Tweeting about your business.

Getting Started with Twitter

I f you already have a Twitter account, feel free to skip this section, but you may want to skim through the section on optimizing your profile. I'll be explaining how to write a compelling profile summary that will grab the attention of people who are thinking of following you.

Signing up for Twitter is really easy and only takes a few minutes. I'll take you through the signup process and show you some tricks I've learned over the years.

CREATING YOUR TWITTER ACCOUNT

Figure 3–1 on page 24 shows you the initial Twitter login/signup screen.

If you are already signed up for Twitter, you can log in on this screen and I'll show you how to optimize your Twitter account so you can attract more followers; and we'll get more in depth with that in Chapter 4. If you don't have a Twitter account, go ahead and enter your full name, email, and the password you want to use for Twitter. Make sure you use a unique, hard-to-guess password so your Twitter account won't get hacked. You wouldn't believe how many people use passwords like *twitter*, *twitter123*, *123456*, *password*, or my favorite, *qwerty*. If your Twitter account gets hacked it can embarrass you or your business, so make sure you use a secure password and change it at least twice a year.

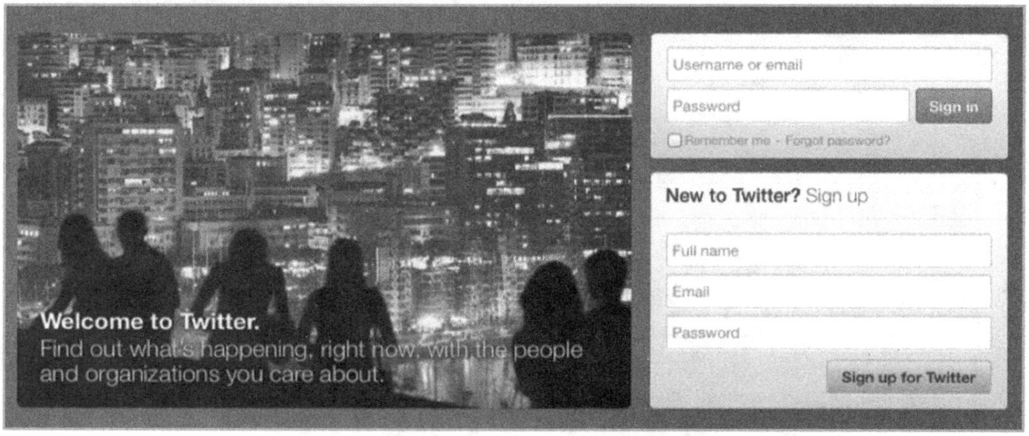

FIGURE 3–1. The Twitter Login/Signup Screen

After you enter your secure password, click on the Sign up for Twitter button and you will see the screen as shown in Figure 3–2. Twitter will let you know if they think your password is secure enough. As you see, I entered a simple password for this test account.

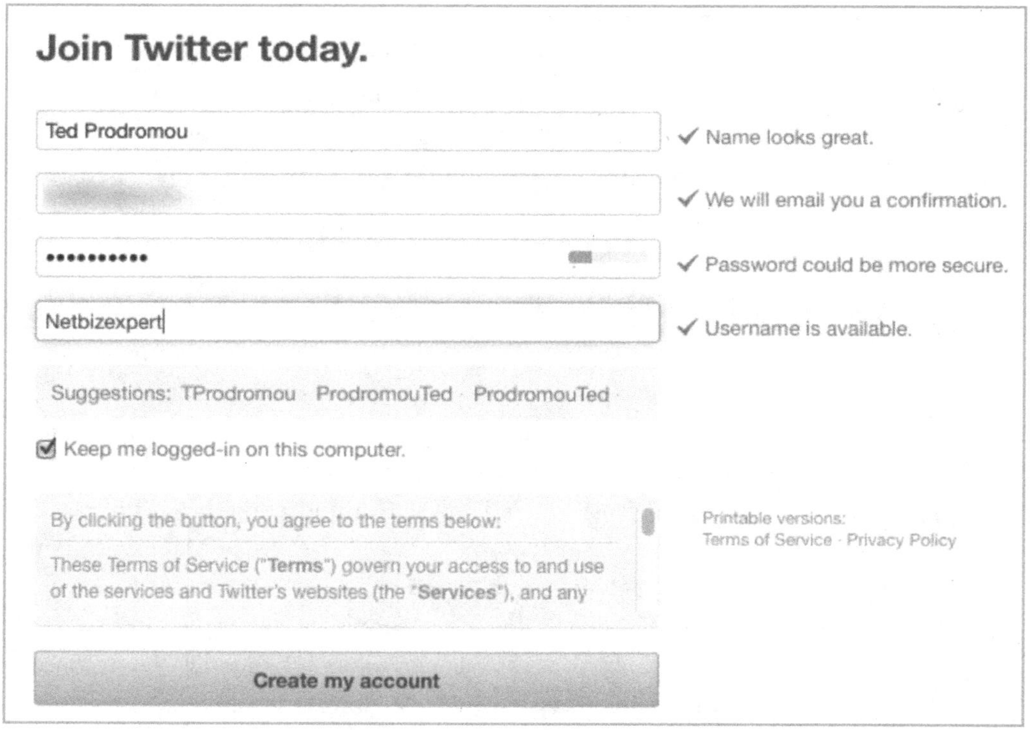

FIGURE 3–2. The Twitter Signup Page Continued

This is the screen where you choose your Twitter name or handle. If you own a business, you should enter your business name here if it's available. You want your Twitter account to be closely associated with your brand name so it's easy for people to find you. If your business name isn't available, try to come up with a very close variation. You have 15 characters to work with and Twitter will make suggestions for you. The Twitter suggestions aren't always the greatest, but they can give you ideas that may trigger some good variations.

If you are a consultant, you'll want to use your business name or your full name. Let Twitter suggest alternatives if your first choice is already taken, and choose a name that is easy for your clients to remember. Don't add numbers to your username unless it helps your clients remember your Twitter handle. I was never a fan of the AOL email addresses where they encouraged you to add numbers to your email address. If I was tedpro427@aol.com, how would anyone know to send email to that address? The same goes for your Twitter handle. Does @tedpro427 mean anything to you? If you know me, you would know to search for @tedprodromou to see if it was me. That's why I always sign up for new social networks when they first launch so I can grab my preferred username. Even if I end up not using the social network much, I have my preferred username of tedprodromou. If the social network takes off and I end up using it, my clients know to look for me as *tedprodromou*. There are other Ted Prodromous out there who are active on social media, so I like to claim my preferred name quickly. I recommend you grab your preferred username as soon as possible on all social media sites so you present a consistent brand to your clients and prospects.

After you select your preferred Twitter handle, click on *Create my Account* and your Twitter account will be created automatically. You will be redirected to the screen shown in Figure 3–3 on page 26, where you will see a sample Tweet as your account is being created.

Now Twitter is going to prompt you many times to start following people. Resist the temptation to start following Ashton Kutcher or Kim Kardashian right now. I know you want to see what all the excitement about Twitter is, but hold on for a few more minutes while we complete your profile.

I think it's really important for you to fill out your profile completely, customize your Twitter page, and have a few Tweets under your belt so they show up on your timeline before you start following people. When you follow someone, they receive an email notification. Chances are they're going to click on your profile and check you out. If your profile is empty and you have the default Twitter picture on your page, you'll look like a potential spammer, blowing your chances of them following you back. Figure 3–4 on page 26 is the first screen that entices you to start following people. Resist the urge to start following these celebrities!

FIGURE 3–3. The Screen You See as Your Twitter Account Is Being Created

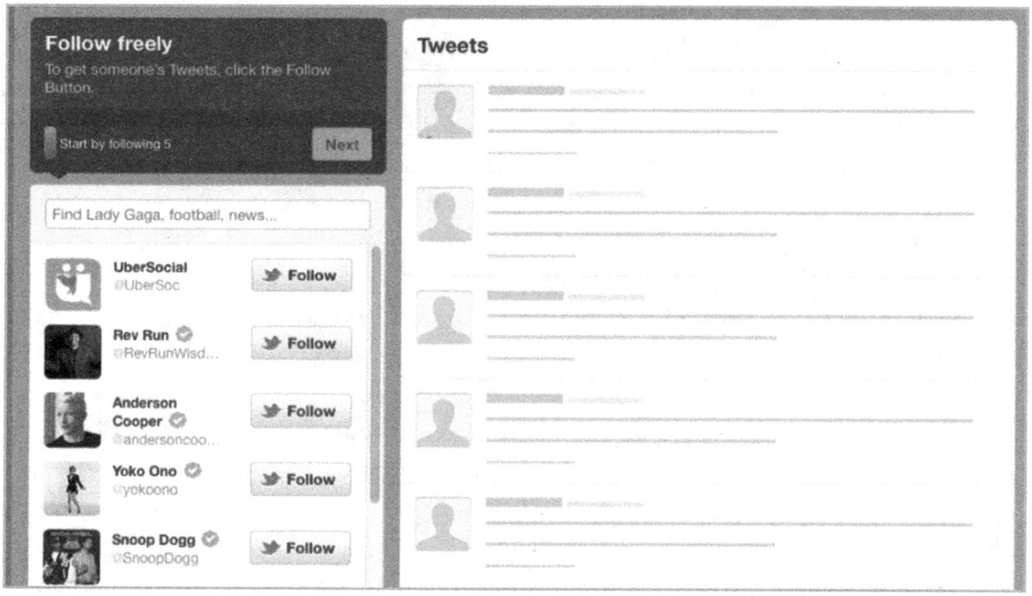

FIGURE 3–4. Twitter Prompts You to Start Following Five Celebrities. Resist the Temptation and Click Skip this Step So You Can Complete Your Profile.

Twitter says to *Start by following 5* but I prefer to *Skip this step* and finish my profile setup. Twitter is going to introduce you to categories in the next step of the setup process. Figure 3–5 on page 27 introduces you to Twitter categories where you can search for people to follow in specific niches.

FIGURE 3–5. Twitter Introduces You to Categories in the Setup Process

Twitter is persistent and asks *Try 5 more* but I still prefer to *Skip this step* and wait to start following people until after I've completed the setup of my profile. The setup wizard continues to walk you through the setup process and will invite you to search through your email contact lists and invite your friends to follow you on Twitter, as shown in Figure 3–6 on page 28.

Now Twitter wants you to search through your email contacts so you can send an automated email inviting them to follow you on Twitter. See Figure 3–6 to see how you would search your email address books and invite your friends to join you on Twitter. I've never been a big fan of these automated invitations, so *Skip this step* for now. You'll start following people after you complete your profile setup and send a few Tweets.

Oh, we're getting so close to finishing!! When you reach the screen shown in Figure 3–7 on page 28 you're almost done with your Twitter account setup. Now you can confirm your email address to complete the initial setup of your profile.

As you see in Figure 3–7, your timeline is empty because you haven't followed anyone yet and you haven't sent your first Tweet. This is why I prefer to complete my profile before I start following people. Many times, people will check out your Twitter profile after you follow them. If they see an empty profile page with no information

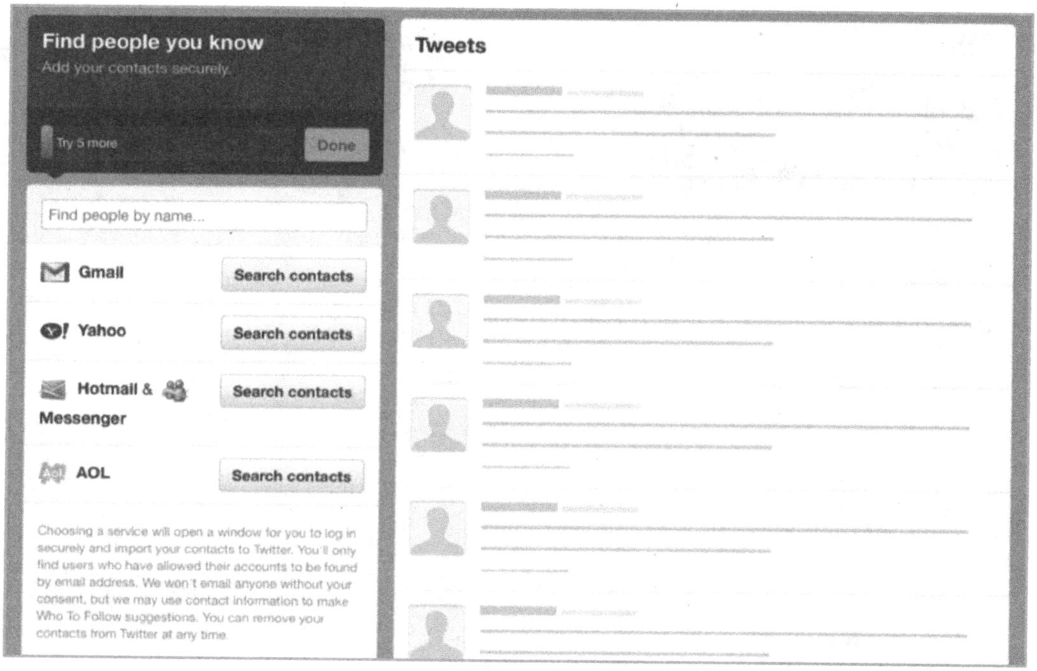

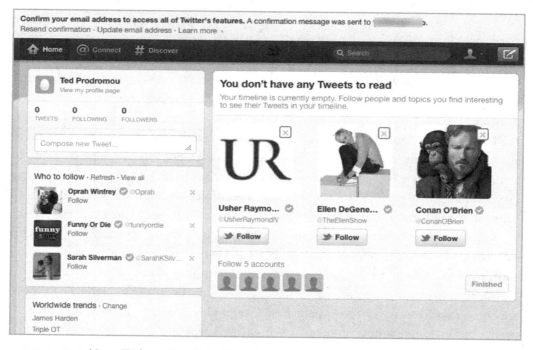

FIGURE 3–6. The Setup Process Continues! It's Time to Invite Your Friends to Follow You on Twitter.

FIGURE 3–7. Your Twitter Setup Is Complete Once You Confirm Your Email Address

about you or Tweets, they may decide not to follow you. When you follow celebrities, the chances of them following you back are somewhere between slim and none so you don't have to worry about them seeing your empty profile page. If you are trying to build a strong group of followers to promote your business, you want to complete your profile first before you start following them. It would be like opening your brick-and-mortar store when it was half built and not ready for business. Potential customers would come in and see a bunch of construction workers building your store and wonder why you were open for business.

Figure 3–8 shows you what your new Twitter page looks like. Now it's time to customize it so you present a professional image to your customers.

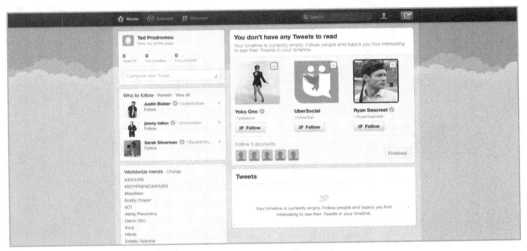

FIGURE 3–8. Your New Twitter Homepage

TWEETING WITH THE OTHER BIRDS

It really comes down to only six actions when using Twitter.

- Tweet a message to the Twitterverse
- Reply to a Tweet
- ReTweet a Tweet
- Send a Direct Message to someone
- Follow someone
- Unfollow someone

Once you master these six actions you are a member of the Twitterati!

TYPES OF TWEETS

Ever wondered where your reply to someone else's Tweet shows up on Twitter? In this section, I will show you the specific types of Tweets and where they will appear on Twitter. Hopefully this gives you a better understanding of where your Tweets go after you click "Tweet."

Normal Tweet

- *Definition*: Any message with fewer than 140 characters posted to Twitter
- *Where it appears for the sender*: On the sender's profile page and Tweets timeline
- *Where it appears for the recipient*: In the Tweets timeline view of anyone who is following the sender
- *Places it will never appear*: On anyone else's profile page, unless they ReTweeted the message

Figure 3–9 shows a normal Tweet from me to my followers.

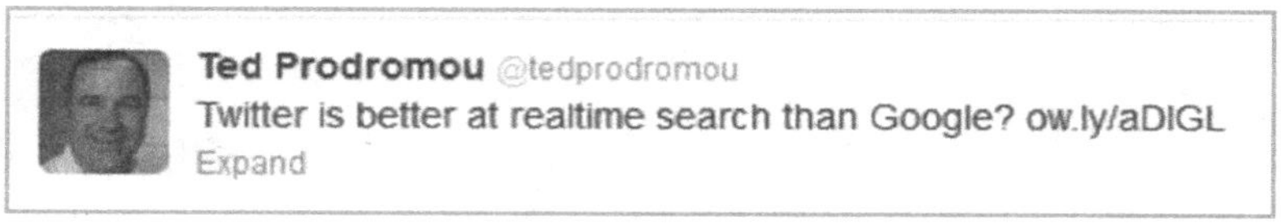

Ted Prodromou @tedprodromou
Twitter is better at realtime search than Google? ow.ly/aDIGL
Expand

FIGURE 3–9. A Normal Tweet from Me

Mentions

- *Definition*: A Tweet containing another user's Twitter username, preceded by the @ symbol, like this: *Hello @tedprodromou! What's up?*
- *Where it appears for the sender*: On the sender's profile page of public Tweets
- *Where it appears for the recipient*: In the recipient's Mentions and Interactions tabs (under the @ Connect tab) on their profile page. Mentions will also appear in the recipient's Tweets timeline view (but not on their profile) if they are following the sender. Note: Anyone on Twitter who is following the sender of a Mention will see the Tweet in their home timeline.
- *Places it will never appear*: On anyone's profile page, unless they wrote the message

Figure 3–10 on page 31 shows you what you will see on your Mention tab when someone includes your Twitter handle in their Tweet. This will also show up when they reply to one of your Tweets.

Carrie Wilkerson @CarrieWilkerson   28 Apr
@tedprodromou wahoooo! enjoy! Now you will 'hear it' in my accent since we've chatted, LOL
💬 View conversation

FIGURE 3–10. A Mention from @CarrieWilkerson after I Purchased her Book

@Replies

- *Definition*: A Tweet that begins with another user's username and is in reply to one of their Tweets, like this: @tedprodromou What do you mean the Giants are going to win the World Series?
- *Where it appears for the sender*: On the sender's Profile page
- *Where it appears for the recipient*: In the recipient's Mentions and Interactions tabs (found under Connect). Like mentions, @replies will also appear in the recipient's Tweets timeline view if they are following the sender. Anyone following the sender and the recipient of an @reply will see it in their Tweets timeline.
- *Places it will never appear*: On anyone's profile page, unless they wrote/sent the message

Figure 3–11 shows you what a reply to one of your Tweets will look like.

Kimberly McCabe @kimberlymccabe   25 Apr
@tedprodromou lol! You know I have to do it. When tempted to see how many points I could get on foursquare
💬 View conversation   ↰ Reply   ⇄ Retweet   ★ Favorite

FIGURE 3–11. A Twitter Reply Will Appear Like This. You Can View the Entire Conversation by Clicking on View Conversation.

Direct Messages

- *Definition*: A personal message sent directly to someone who follows you or sent directly to you from someone you follow
- *Where it appears for the sender*: In the sender's Direct Messages (accessible by clicking on the person icon in the upper-right corner). A DM (direct message) will disappear if the recipient deletes it.
- *Where it appears for the recipient*: In the recipient's Direct Messages. Will disappear if the sender deletes it.
- *Places it will never appear*: In any public timeline or public search

PROTECTED TWEETS

If you don't want to share your Tweets with the entire Twitterverse, you can protect your Tweets so only authorized people can see them. This option is good if you are working with a team you want to communicate with privately. If you want to use Protected Tweets, I recommend setting up a separate Twitter account. That way you can still use your primary Twitter account to interact with other Twitter users.

When you protect your Tweets, the following restrictions are put in place:

- People will have to request to follow you; each follow request will need approval.
- Your Tweets will only be visible to users you've approved.
- Other users will not be able to ReTweet your Tweets.
- Protected Tweets will not appear in Twitter search or Google search.
- @replies you send to people who aren't following you will not be seen by those users (because you have not given them permission to see your Tweets).
- You cannot share permanent links to your Tweets with anyone other than your approved followers.

To turn Protected Tweets on, go to your Twitter Settings as you see in Figure 3–12 and check the box next to Protect my Tweets.

FIGURE 3–12. Enabling the Protect My Tweets Feature So Your Tweets Do Not Appear Publicly

WHY ONLY 140 CHARACTERS?

A lot of people are frustrated that they only get 140 characters for their Tweets. Others love the brevity of Tweets because the messages have to be short and sweet. There's no fluff or run-on sentences in Twitter.

Did you know a Tweet is actually 160 characters? I didn't know this bit of trivia until the other day. Here's the explanation from the 2008 Twitter FAQ about the origin of the character limit.

We like to keep it short and sweet! It also just so happens that 140 characters is the perfect length for sending status updates via text message. The standard text message length in most

places is 160 characters per message. We reserve 20 characters for people's names, and the other 140 are all yours!

WHAT SHOULD I SAY?

This is the number-one reason people dislike Twitter. I don't know if they get writer's block or freak out because they only have 140 characters to work with. I struggled with this, too, so you are not alone if you don't know what to say. Look at my first Tweet, "making friends" if you're worried about making a fool of yourself. My lame first Tweet didn't make me lose any clients or have any tragic negative effects on my business. I bet nobody ever saw my first Tweet because I didn't have any followers and I was only following a few people at that point. Remember there are over 340 million Tweets per day, so your chances people will see your initial Tweets are about the same as getting struck by lightning.

Tweets are like the subject lines of your emails. What do you put in your subject line when you are sending an email to a friend or when you are sending out your monthly e-zine? Experts say shorter email subject lines are more effective than long subject lines. A good email subject line is usually less than 100 characters. Use the same thought process when you are sending a Tweet, and in no time you will get over your fear of Tweeting.

Tweeting for business is different than Tweeting from your personal account, which is why I recommend setting up one Twitter account for your business and another account for personal use. Keep your business Tweeting professional so you project a professional image. It's okay to add a little humor or even a little controversy to your business Tweets, but don't go overboard. You want to make your business Tweets interesting and compelling so people will want to follow you and click on the links you add to your Tweets, but you don't want to offend people with unprofessional behavior.

If you are still stuck, here are some ideas to help you create Tweets that your followers will enjoy.

Read Other People's Tweets and Copy What They Are Doing

This is the easiest and most obvious thing to do. Follow some popular business Twitter users like @chrisbrogan, @petershankman, @timoreilly, @marismith, @briansolis, @ susanroane, and @garyvee. There are many other great Twitter users you can learn from, but these are some of the top business-related Twitter users. You can find other people to follow using the # Discover tab in your Twitter account where you can find Twitter users in any category under the Browse Categories tab. Figure 3–13 on page 34 shows you how to find people to follow in different categories.

FIGURE 3–13. Finding Popular Twitter Users to Follow So You Can See
What They Tweet About

You can start by ReTweeting and adding your comments or thoughts to the Tweet. When you ReTweet a business leader's Tweet, people subconsciously associate you with the person, adding to your credibility. You may not know that business leader now, but they will appreciate the fact that you took the time to ReTweet their message and added your own perspective. If you continually ReTweet another expert's Tweets and add value, often that person will reach out to you and start ReTweeting your Tweets. How powerful would it be if @chrisbrogan or @briansolis started ReTweeting your Tweets?

Tweet Breaking News

Twitter is the first place you find breaking news from around the world, whether it's related to politics, business, sports, or natural disasters. You can follow popular media outlets like

@cnnbreak, @nytimes, or others, and ReTweet breaking events, or create new Tweets with links to their news items. You will be helping tell your Twitterverse about breaking news and people will know you are someone who keeps up with current events. You can also Tweet about breaking news in your industry, which will add to your credibility.

Don't forget to add hashtags to your Tweets so people on Twitter who are not following you but monitoring hashtags will see your Tweets. When Steve Jobs passed away millions of people sent their prayers and condolences by adding the hashtag #stevejobs to their Tweets. That hashtag became a trending topic so millions of Twitter users knew he'd passed minutes after it was announced.

Be a Curator

We all read articles about our industry and profession on the internet. As you come across interesting or controversial news stories related to your business or industry, Tweet a link to that article. In the Tweet, tell your followers what you liked or disliked about the article. Adding your perspective adds value for your followers.

You don't have to Tweet only articles you agree with. When you disagree with an article, you should let your followers know so they see where you stand on the subject. Disagreeing in your Tweet can lead to many stimulating Twitter conversations with your followers and the conversation will often expand outside your Twitterverse, expanding your following.

Don't forget to add relevant hashtags to these Tweets to expand the reach of your Tweet.

Help Requests

One of the most popular uses of Twitter is to reach out for support. Every day people Tweet to find solutions to their problems.

You can monitor popular hashtags or keywords related to your products or your industry and help people when they have questions. When you Reply to their Tweets to help them, people will see you are an expert in that area. You can send links to webpages that can solve their problem or make suggestions in your Tweets. They will be grateful to you for helping them.

You can also ask other Twitter users for help when you have a problem. You can Tweet something like, "Is anyone else having a problem with #Firefox crashing since the last update?" Notice how I turned "Firefox" into a hashtag so nonfollowers will see the question and be able to reach out. You will be surprised to see how fast people respond to your help requests.

Say Thank You

Nothing feels better than someone thanking you after you help them. The next time someone helps you, whether it's online or offline, thank them on Twitter and word will spread quickly. Let's say your neck and shoulders are super tight because you've been working on a huge project at work. You've been working on your computer for 12 hours a day for weeks and you can barely turn your head. You get a fantastic massage and feel a thousand times better. You can thank your masseuse on Twitter by Tweeting "Thanks @*masseuse* [your masseuse's Twitter handle] for the fabulous massage #BestMassageEver www.*masseuse.com* [the website].

You will be telling everyone on Twitter that you just received a great massage, giving her some free publicity and driving traffic to her website so others can make an appointment. This Tweet will take about 30 seconds for you to do and your masseuse will be incredibly grateful.

Evaluations, Reviews, and Opinions of New Products or Services

When you are thinking about purchasing a new product or service, you can use Twitter Search to see what others are saying about the product or service. You can join in the conversations by replying to their review of the product or ask them questions.

When you purchase new products or services, you can share your opinion with others on Twitter. Include a relevant hashtag so more Twitter users will see your review.

A sample Tweet could be, "Just bought the new iPad. Love the faster speed and incredible display. Don't like the extra weight though. #iPad"

Resend Great Content

If you come across a great article or useful tip that isn't time sensitive, go ahead and Tweet it again even if you Tweeted it in the past. Don't repeat the Tweet if you just Tweeted it recently, but it may be worth Tweeting it again a month or two later. I don't recommend Tweeting about articles or content that is time sensitive and the content isn't relevant anymore.

Share Your Thoughts

Be careful with this one because some people overdo it. They share their inner voice with the Twitterverse, often sharing too much information.

People do like to hear what's on your mind occasionally. This helps build a stronger relationship with your followers and lets them know you have problems and vulnerabilities, too. We all have things that drive us crazy in life and it's good to vent occasionally.

Have Fun

It's OK to let your guard down and Tweet some fun things like jokes, famous quotes, and links to funny videos, or lyrics from a song that's stuck in your head. This lets people know you are human and have a fun side to you in addition to your business expertise. This goes a long way to strengthening the bond between you and your followers.

These are Tweets you can schedule in advance to fill in the times when you aren't Tweeting. I like to schedule Tweets like this in the evening or on weekends to let people know I don't work 24/7. I recommend sending Tweets like this about 20 percent of the time to break up the seriousness of your business-related Tweets.

Be a Connector

Twitter can also be used for business networking. You can introduce one of your colleagues to another colleague via an online introduction on Twitter. This is very powerful because it shows your followers that you are well connected and are willing to introduce your followers to each other when it's appropriate.

A good time to make mass recommendations is on Fridays by adding either #FollowFriday or #FF to your Tweets. You Tweet a list of your followers that you would recommend to others so it goes out to the entire Twitterverse with the #FollowFriday hashtag, which is one of the most followed hashtags.

Promote Your Company

You can Tweet links about your company. Some of the most popular topics people Tweet about are:

- A new blog post
- Client acquisitions
- Press releases
- Jobs available
- Awards/recognition
- Events you're hosting and/or are attending
- Discussions you're hosting on LinkedIn
- Special offers, sales or discounts

As you see, there are so many things you can share on Twitter.

WHAT NOT TO SAY ON TWITTER

Now that you have some ideas what you *can* say on Twitter, let's talk about what you shouldn't say. We've all put our foot in our mouth and said the wrong thing to someone.

I'm sure it was embarrassing and you may have heard about it from a few people who overheard your misspoken comment. It probably went no further than the few people who were in the room when you made your embarrassing remark, unless you did it on national TV in front of millions of people.

When you say the wrong thing on social media it's not only visible to millions of people, it stays online for a long time. Maybe someone doesn't see your embarrassing Tweet when you sent it, but it can show up in a Google search months, or even years, later. You need to think twice, maybe three times, before you press the Tweet button if you are responding to someone who has upset you. Sending a Tweet in anger rarely ends in a good result. Take a few deep breaths, count to ten and ask yourself if you want the entire world to read what you are about to Tweet.

Never respond in a negative way when someone says something on social media that has upset you. If you do respond, do it in a diplomatic way, because the Twitterverse is watching. Responding in a professional way has a positive effect on your reputation, while responding in a negative way will make you look immature to your followers and will have a negative effect on your business. Many of you have your Twitter account connected to your Facebook and LinkedIn accounts so your Tweets appear on all three networks. Do you want your negative Tweet to appear on LinkedIn, where your customers and prospects can see it?

Think about why you are using social media for your business. You aren't using social media to air your dirty laundry to your customers. You are doing it to grow your business.

When considering using social media for your business, you should keep three important things in mind:

1. *Have a purpose.* We'll talk about creating your Twitter strategy in Chapter 5. For now, start thinking about why you are using social media for your business. Is it to generate leads, monitor your brand, provide support to your customers, or to expand your professional network? If you are just starting out with Twitter, "listen" to other conversations until you get comfortable with the way conversations flow. Don't Tweet anything you wouldn't say to someone in person.

2. *It isn't all about you.* Don't send an endless stream of Tweets about you and your company. Twitter works best when you engage others in conversation, just like when you meet people in person. People love to be thanked on Twitter.

   Have you ever read *How to Win Friends and Influence People* by Dale Carnegie, or *How to Work a Room* by Susan RoAne? If you haven't read these fantastic networking books, I highly recommend you do so as soon as you finish this book. Both teach you how to walk into a room where you know absolutely nobody and instantly connect with everyone you meet.

Twitter works exactly the same way as in-person networking. Do you want to know the secret? The secret is to be more interested in learning about others than you are in telling them all about you. People will instantly connect with you if you show interest in them and ask them questions about where they work, what they do for a living, or what they love to do in their spare time. Ask them a question and listen to their answer. Ask them another question and just listen. Let them do 80 percent of the talking and they will walk away telling their friends that you are the most interesting person they met in a long time.

Do the same on Twitter. Ask someone a question and listen to their answer. You could get my attention by Tweeting something like "Hey @tedprodromou, what's your favorite restaurant in San Francisco?" I would check out your Twitter profile if I didn't know you to learn more about you. I would reply with my favorite restaurant and probably ask you what your favorite restaurant is. If you hadn't shown interest in me, I probably never would have seen your Tweets on Twitter because I don't follow monologue Tweeters. I call people monologue Tweeters if they just send Tweets and never reply to other people's Tweets or

THE UNTWEETABLES

Here are some tips for topics you should avoid Tweeting about. I know these may seem obvious to you, but every day people Tweet about them and they reflect negatively on their business.

- Don't say negative things about your competition.

- Don't engage your competition in negative conversations.

- Don't get into fights with angry customers online. Engage them by asking them how you can help them and invite them to email you or call you for assistance.

- Don't Tweet about your sex life.

- Don't Tweet about wild nights out and definitely don't Tweet pictures of your wild night out.

- Don't Tweet about politics.

- Don't Tweet about religion.

interact with others. If you look at these persons' timelines, they look like a one-way conversation.

3. *Remember your clients and your mother.* I see this tip frequently in social media guides. Don't post anything you wouldn't want your mother, grandmother, clients, or employees to read and associate with you. Word travels fast on the internet and your posts can be ReTweeted and forwarded to millions in seconds.

Remember you are using Twitter to promote your business, so you want to be professional at all times. It's OK to engage others in conversation, but don't get into controversial topics that can polarize your customers and prospects.

YOUR FIRST TWEET

We've laid the groundwork. Your Twitter profile is complete, and you are following some people. You know the Twitter commands and you know what not to say, so it's time for your first Tweet. I gave you some ideas about what you can Tweet, so let's do it!

Are you going to Tweet a link to a blog post? Are you going to ReTweet someone's Tweet that you liked? You want your first Tweet to be memorable like your first kiss, so take a few minutes to create a message you'll be proud of. Don't be lame like me and say something stupid!

You can see what other people Tweeted for their first Tweet on sites like www.twopcharts.com. Just enter their Twitter handle and you can see their first ten Tweets or their last 3200 Tweets if they've Tweeted more than 3200 times, their first ten followers, and the first ten Twitter users they followed.

If you can't think of anything clever or memorable, you can even just let people know you are just getting started on Twitter and share your excitement.

Ready, set, GO!

See, that didn't hurt, did it?

Take a screenshot of your first Tweet and save it. You'll enjoy reading it in a few years after you've Tweeted a few thousand times.

CONCLUSION

Your Twitter account is now ready to use. Feel free to start following people and Tweeting. Start logging into Twitter a few times a day so you incorporate it into your work routine. Think about the time you spend on Twitter as part of your business marketing. In the next chapter, we're going to customize your Twitter profile so it matches your business brand and is optimized so you can attract the right followers.

Chapter 4

Customizing Your Twitter Profile to Attract Followers

Now we get into the fun part of setting up your Twitter profile. There are a few important factors that will entice someone to follow you: your name, picture, biography, Tweets, and followers. I'll show you how to optimize each "follow factor" so you can build a quality Twitter community for your business.

We already talked about the importance of a good Twitter name. You want it to be catchy, easy to remember, and related to your business whether you are a consultant or own a small business. You don't want to use hard-to-remember acronyms or names with letters and numbers unless they are directly related to your business.

YOUR TWITTER PROFILE PICTURE

If you are using Twitter for personal interactions only, feel free to use any crazy picture you want on your profile. Because you are using Twitter to promote your business, however, I strongly suggest using a business-appropriate picture in your profile. Your Twitter profile is your personal brand and you are the face of your business, so no pictures of you at Burning Man after a week without a bath or a picture of you at a pre-football game tailgate party drinking shots of tequila. Don't use a picture of yourself in kindergarten or a picture of your cat, either. Nobody

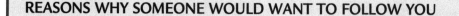

REASONS WHY SOMEONE WOULD WANT TO FOLLOW YOU

- They like your Twitter name or handle

- They like your Twitter picture

- They like your Twitter bio

- They like your Tweets

- You have a large number of people following you

cares what you looked like as a 5-year-old and people get their cat fixes on YouTube. Occasionally I see people post pictures of their children as their profile picture. I highly recommend not posting pictures of your young children on the internet anywhere for safety reasons. There are many child preditors on the internet and you want to protect your children.

It's not bad to use a casual picture of yourself for your Twitter profile. In fact, I think you *should* use a casual picture of yourself for Twitter, because it's a casual environment. If your business is targeted toward a more professional audience, a business-casual photo would work fine. I believe you would look out of place if you used a picture of yourself in a business suit or formal attire, but that's just my opinion. Look at the profile pictures of other people in your profession and see what kind of photo they use to get an idea of what looks best.

You should always use a high-quality picture in which you are smiling and looking friendly. You want to start with a high-quality picture so it doesn't look blurry or grainy when you crop and resize it. Headshots are fine and work best, because Twitter crops your picture to 73 by 73 pixels. It's hard to get much more than your head in a 73 x 73 image.

Don't take your picture using your cell phone camera held at arm's length or with a web cam. Most photos you take of yourself at arm's length are off center, out of focus, or show you with a strange look on your face as you extend your arm and lean back a little to fit into the picture. Web cams are great for video conferencing, but the pictures they take aren't the best quality. Get a friend to take some good pictures of you with different backgrounds so you get a variety of photos to choose from. Make sure the background isn't too busy because it will distract from the main focus of the picture—you. If you have a busy background you may blend in with it and get lost in the photo or it may even become the primary focus of the photo. Remember, this photo is all about you because you are your personal brand, which is so important in social media. Figure 4–1 shows you a great scenery picture but you would barely notice me in Figure 4–2 if I used this as my profile picture.

FIGURE 4–1. Great Scenery Picture

FIGURE 4–2. But a Terrible Profile Picture

Figure 4–3 on page 44 is an example of a bad profile image for a small-business owner. Your prospects and customers want to get to know and trust you. If you are unwilling to post an image of yourself, they may become suspicious and not trust you enough to do business with you.

If you are using Twitter to promote your business, don't use a caricature or cartoon image of yourself for your profile photo unless you really are an illustrator or cartoonist. People want to do business with real people, not cartoon characters.

People often ask me if it's OK to use their business logo as their profile photo. If your Twitter name is your brand name, then of course you should use your logo

FIGURE 4–3. A Poor Choice for Your Twitter Profile Picture

as your profile photo. It would look awkward if @walmart used a picture of a person as their profile photo. It would also look awkward if I used my company logo for my @tedprodromou profile. People want to get to know Ted Prodromou if I am Tweeting from @tedprodromou.

Take some time now to look at other profile pictures of people who are the same age as you and in the same industry or business. This will give you a sense of what type of profile picture you should use. You want your profile picture to be unique so you stand out from the crowd but you want to maintain a professional but casual image.

How often should you change your profile picture? It's a matter of personal preference, but I like to change up my social media profile pictures every few months to get people to notice my profile and to show different sides of me. I prefer to show more current photos of myself instead of showing photos of me from 20 years ago, when I was a little lighter and had much darker hair. I prefer the "full disclosure" approach because some day you may meet some of your followers in person and they will be shocked when they see you much older than your profile picture. I think this is important if you are a consultant, instructor, or public speaker, because you don't want to deceive your followers into thinking you are much younger than you really are. They will instantly lose trust in you and probably never want to do business with you.

IMAGE BANNERS

Twibbon, www.twibbon.com, is a website where you can create banners you overlay onto your profile photo to let others know you are supporting a cause, such as breast cancer or Lance Armstrong's Livstrong Foundation. You can also create Twibbons to protest political causes, to promote events, show your support for your favorite sports teams, or even show what country you are from. The Twibbons are usually small and unobtrusive so they don't distract users from seeing your smiling face. I think Twibbons are a great way to let others know you support causes like cancer research or other charitable foundations, but I do not think it's appropriate for you to share your political beliefs on your Twitter profile photo unless you are a politician or are involved in politics. If your favorite sports team is in the baseball World Series or your favorite football team is in the Super Bowl, I don't see any harm in letting others know you are a sports fan and you support your local teams. It's a great way to let others know a little bit more about you. After the big sporting event is over and you've relished your team's victory for a week or so, I do recommend removing the sports-related Twibbon.

YOUR TWITTER BIO

Twitter gives you 160 characters to tell the world why they should follow you. Remember, your bio is essentially a Tweet that compels people to want to follow you. Your Twitter bio is like an extended headline that grabs the attention of the person viewing your profile. People will follow you if they have similar interests as you and/or they can learn something from you.

There are many different approaches people use to create compelling bios. Unfortunately most people don't put much thought into their bios, which can cause a lot of people not to follow you. You are using Twitter to promote and grow your business, so you need to put some thought into it so you can attract as many followers as possible. Think of your Twitter bio as a Google Ad. When people see your Google Ad, you have one chance to grab their attention and get them to click on your ad or you lose them forever. Use the same approach when writing your Twitter bio so the viewer can't resist following you.

So what should you put in your Twitter bio?

Twitter Bio Content Ideas

Your objective is to get as many like-minded people to follow you and/or your business as you can so they will become raving fans and spread the word about you to their friends. Some of the ways to create a compelling Twitter bio are:

- *Share your interests in your bio.* Let the viewers know what you are passionate about, such as music, art, sports, travel, hiking, skiing, etc. This lets them get to know the personal side of you, which builds a stronger relationship with your followers.
- *Let people know what you are about.* Sharing your goals or life vision can be a powerful statement that will grab their attention. For example, if you are passionate about work/life balance and you value your family life more than your work, let

readers know. You will attract many faithful followers by letting people know where you stand on important issues, but stay away from politics and religion unless you only want clients that belong to one political party or one religious belief. There is nothing more polarizing than discussing politics or religion with someone who deviates from your belief. This can turn off a lot of potential followers or prospective customers immediately.

- *Share your areas of expertise.* If you are an expert C++ programmer, a highly successful internet marketer, have over 20 years' experience as a CPA, or are a master woodworker, include that information in your Twitter bio. People follow experts so they can learn from them.
- *Share your passions if you are a coach, teacher, or consultant.* A great example would be, "I'm passionate about helping small-business owners make more money. Follow me to learn how." How many small-business owners would follow you if that were in your bio? Every small-business owner wants to make more money, so of course they're going to follow you to receive your tips.
- *A series of keywords will grab potential followers' attention.* People search for keyword phrases on Twitter just like they do on Google. Let's say you're a personal trainer. If someone on Twitter is looking for a personal trainer who can help them lose 20 pounds, they're going to search for great trainers to follow. The keywords you add to your Twitter bio will help you appear in those Twitter searches for "personal trainer." If you're a local business looking for local clients, don't forget to add your city or its initials in your keyword list. For example, you should add "San Francisco personal trainer" to your Twitter bio if you are looking for clients in that city.
- *What makes you different from your competitors?* Every business needs to know the answer to this question. This is commonly known as your unique selling proposition, or USP. There are thousands of small-business marketing consultants on Twitter. Why are you different or better than the others? Let the viewers know why you are different or better in your Twitter bio. This is a very effective way for you to get more people to follow you.
- *Be specific when you are describing your expertise or experience.* Don't just say you are a chiropractor. Let people know you are a "chiropractor with over 20 years of experience relieving people of their neck and back pain." If you are a tech consultant, let them know you are a "Cisco router expert who has worked with Oracle, eBay, Apple, and HP." This is so much more effective than saying, "I'm a network consultant."
- *Have some fun.* Twitter bios are really boring if you just list a bunch of keywords or skills. Show some of your personality with some humor or fun facts about yourself. People want to know you are human in addition to being an expert at what you do.

Remember you only get 160 characters to accomplish this, so spend some time on Twitter.com reviewing the bios of your competitors and people who have a lot of followers to see what approach they are using. You can even get some good ideas from celebrities because they're usually good at showing their personal side in their bios.

Guy Kawasaki (@guykawasaki) is a recognized tech evangelist who uses a different approach. He promotes his book as well as establishing his credibility by sharing his past experience.

> Author of *Enchantment: The Art of Changing Hearts, Minds, and Actions.* Former chief evangelist of Apple. Co-founder of Alltop.

BE REAL IN YOUR BIO

Here's the bio of Katy Perry (@katyperry), the pop star:

> Santa Barbara raised, California gal . . .doing stuff. Working on my mom-esque dance moves in my spare time. How embarrassing.

You get to know a lot about Katy in just a few short statements. You get the feeling she's the "girl next door" who happens to be one of the most famous pop stars today. She also shows a vulnerable side of herself, talking about her mom-esque dance moves.

Chris Brogan (@chrisbrogan) is a recognized social media expert who gives people multiple opportunities to connect with him through his Twitter bio. Notice you can add multiple hyperlinks to your Twitter bio so people can easily connect with you.

> President, Human Business Works. More? *http://bit.ly/cbbio* contact: *http://chrisbrogan.com/contact*

Chris is a recognized expert so he doesn't spend much time educating potential followers about his expertise. This is a great approach once you are established as an expert, but it's not a good approach if you are just trying to establish yourself. You have to share your expertise and build your reputation in your Twitter bio until you reach industry thought-leader status.

Carrie Wilkerson (@carriewilkerson) is a small-business consultant who has used social media to build a thriving work-at-home consulting business so she can be home for her four children. Carrie uses the keyword approach to her Twitter bio.

> Consultant/Strategist for self-employed professionals & small business owners, Wife, Mom, Author, Speaker & Joyful Human! Host of *http://BarefootExecutive.TV*

You know exactly what Carrie does for a living, how she can help you, a bit about her personal life, and a link to her fabulous videos. And you know that she's a joyful human!

Rishi Lakhani (@rishil) uses the story approach in his Twitter bio.

> I am just your average guy interested in SEO and knowing people. This twitter
> a/c is explicitly me and only me. http://explicitly.me

Rishi uses a very simple but compelling statement as his bio and makes it easy for you to visit his site to learn more about him.

If you are a businessperson, you can use the same approach when creating your bio. You can use a series of keywords that describe how you help your clients or you can create a short statement. The key is to clearly communicate how you can help the reader and make it easy for them to connect with you, like @chrisbrogan does.

In Figure 4–4 you see how BLiNQ Media lets you know exactly what they do and how they help agencies and big brands succeed on Facebook.

There is no right or wrong way to write a Twitter bio. Try each approach and see which works best for you. The right approach for you is the one that gets the best results. When you start receiving comments on your bio or see an increase in followers, you'll know you have the right style. I also recommend updating your bio every few months to keep it fresh. Life is constantly evolving, so update your profile to correspond with what's currently going on in your life or your business.

BLiNQ Media ✔
@BLiNQMedia

BLiNQ Media is a Social Engagement Advertising (SM) company that delivers break-through Facebook results for agencies and big brands.
Atlanta GA · http://www.blinqmedia.com

FIGURE 4–4. Blinq Media Has a Clear Bio That Explains What They Do and Who They Help

ADVANCED PROFILE CONFIGURATION

Your basic Twitter profile is now complete, so it's time to get into the advanced profile configuration. To configure your advanced profile settings, log into your Twitter account and click on the icon that looks like the silhouette of a head in the top right corner of your Twitter page. Figure 4–5 on page 49 shows you how to change your Twitter profile settings.

Once you enter the Settings section of your profile you will be able to configure a variety of advanced settings, including your account, password, mobile, notifications,

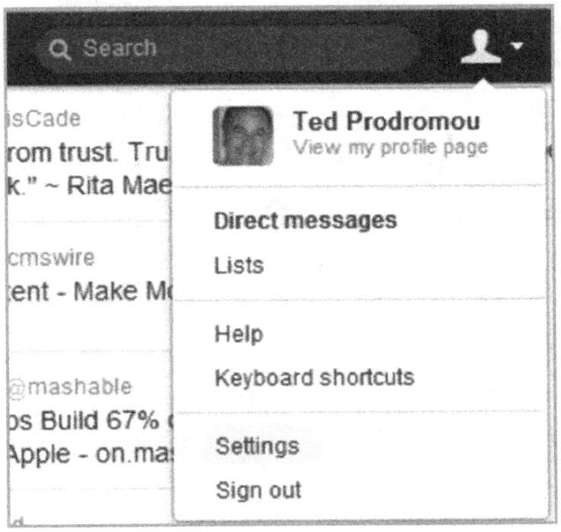

FIGURE 4–5. Changing Your Advanced Twitter Settings

profile, design, and apps, as shown in Figure 4-6. As you see, Twitter gives you a lot of options to customize your Twitter profile so you can stand out from the crowd. Let's go through your configuration options now.

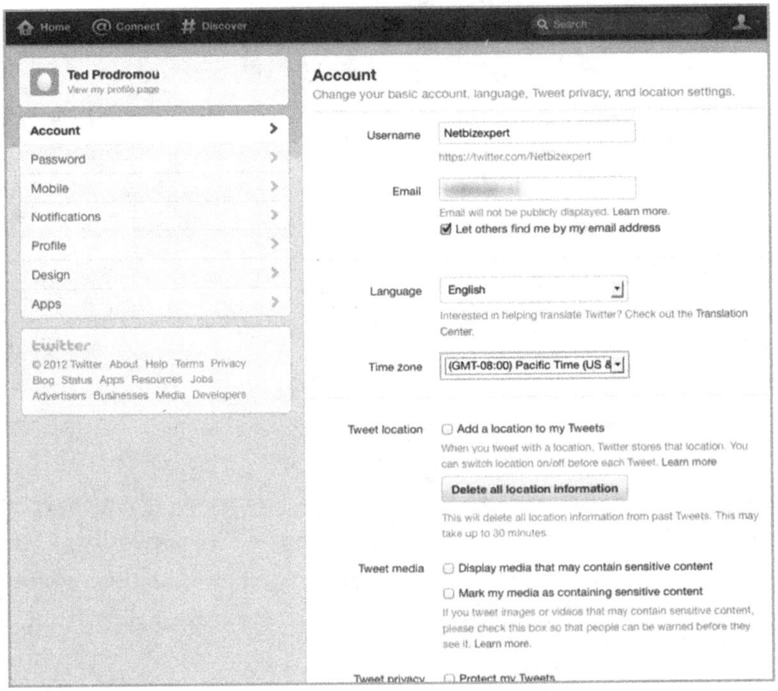

FIGURE 4–6. Your Advanced Twitter Configuration Options

Account

Your username, email, and password settings are created when you sign up for Twitter. If you want to change your Twitter username, you can simply type in your new Twitter name and the system will let you know if it's available. If it is available just click Save at the bottom of the page and your Twitter username will be changed. I changed my Twitter username a few times before I started using Twitter extensively. I don't recommend changing your Twitter username if you have a lot of links on other websites pointing to your Twitter profile. When I changed from www. twitter.com/l3fty to www.twitter.com/tedprodromou, all of the links I posted on other websites that said, "Follow me on Twitter at www.twitter.com/l3fty" became broken links.

I always check the box *Let others find me by my email address* to make it easy for people to find me. After all, isn't the idea of social media to connect with as many like-minded people as possible?

Next, set your language and time zone to the appropriate settings. The next setting, *Add a location to my Tweets,* will let people know where you are Tweeting from. This is useful if you Tweet from different locations, like speaking engagements or conferences. Some people only Tweet from their home or office computer, so this setting doesn't mean much to them.

The Tweet media option lets you warn people that the images or video attached to your Tweet may contain sensitive information. This could include media that is not appropriate for children or may offend a reader in some way. Frankly, I don't see a need to check these boxes because I wouldn't expect a small-business owner to be Tweeting inappropriate media. If there is some reason you might want to Tweet sensitive information to promote your business, then by all means check these boxes so people are warned before they click on your media link.

Tweet privacy lets you keep your Tweets private so only authorized people can read them. This is a great option for people who want to set up a private Twitter network within their company to share information between team members. You could also set up a private support network for your customers so they can receive support reserved for companies with service contracts for your products.

The next option, *Always use HTTPS*, shown in Figure 4–7, page 51, gives you the option of using HTTPS to keep your Tweets secure when possible. This is a good option so your Tweets won't easily be scanned by the automated programs that create the Twitter spam you so often see. It won't protect you completely from appearing in Twitter spam but it does help. Last but not least, select your country, and this section of your Twitter profile is complete.

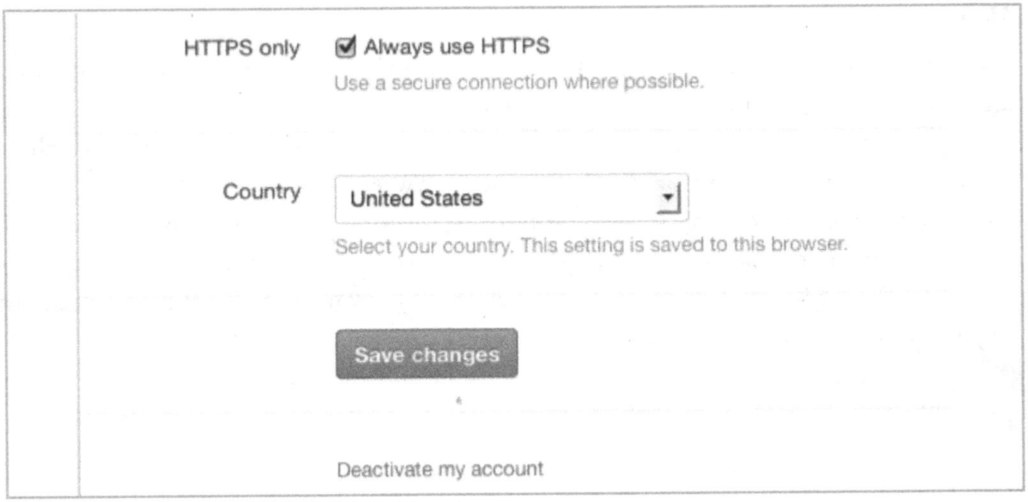

FIGURE 4–7. Always Select HTTPS So Your Twitter Account Will Use a Secure Connection When Possible

Password

The Password tab as seen in Figure 4–8 will let you reset your Twitter password, which I recommend doing every few months. Hackers are always looking for ways to get into your Twitter account. Recently, a company I followed was hacked and the hacker sent direct messages to all of their followers with pornographic images attached. It was very embarrassing for them.

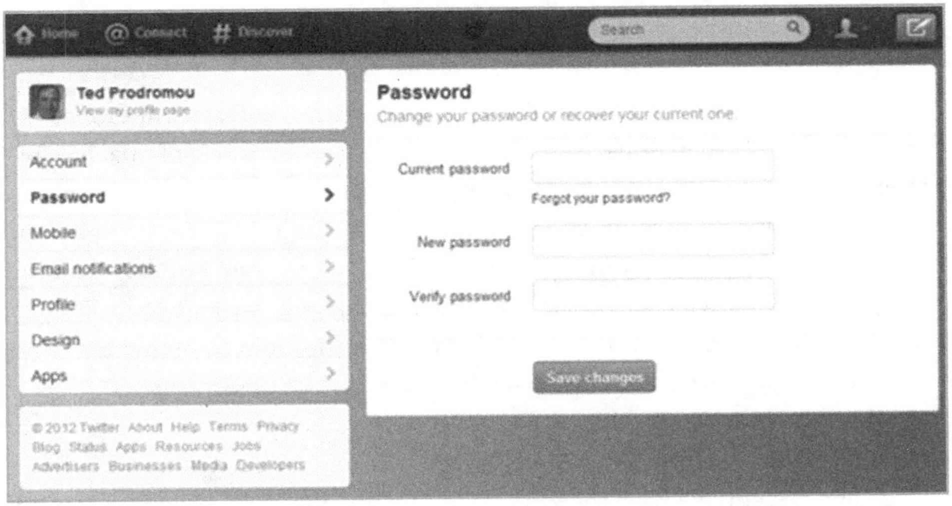

FIGURE 4–8. Changing Your Twitter Password

Mobile

The next tab is the Mobile configuration, as shown in Figure 4–9. Enter your country and mobile phone number so you can send and receive Tweets from your mobile phone. Twitter is a perfect application to use on your mobile devices so you can share information when you are on the go. I always Tweet from my phone when I'm at conferences. I share the important points from the speakers, as well as connect with people at the event. When you send a Tweet from a conference and attach the conference hashtag, others who are attending the conference know you are there and can reach out to you to get together for a meeting or drinks.

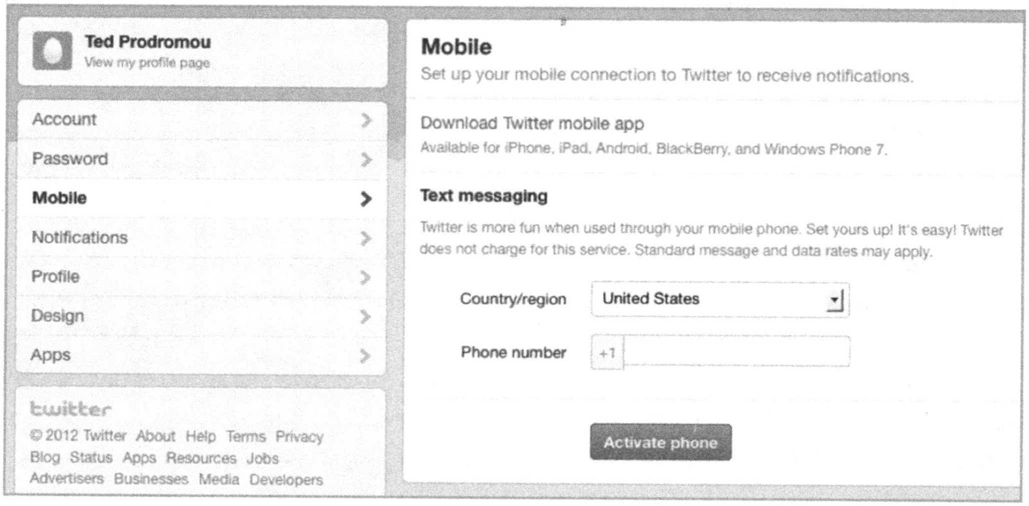

FIGURE 4–9. Configuring Your Mobile Options

Once you enter your mobile number, the configuration options will increase so you can control which notifications will be sent directly to your mobile phone. Figure 4–10 shows you the options for sending notifications directly to your mobile device.

I don't recommend turning on these notifications unless you want to be notified every time someone follows you, mentions you, or ReTweets your Tweets. If you turn on all of these notifications, your phone will be going crazy all day and you will rack up a ton of text messages on your account. The only options I would recommend turning on are *Tweets from people you've enabled for mobile notifications* and *Direct messages.*

I highly recommend installing a Twitter app on your mobile device. I've personally used the official Twitter apps, HootSuite, TweetDeck, and my current favorite, Tweetbot. All of the apps essentially have the same functionality but their user interfaces differ. I suggest testing all of the apps and going with the one that is easiest for you to use.

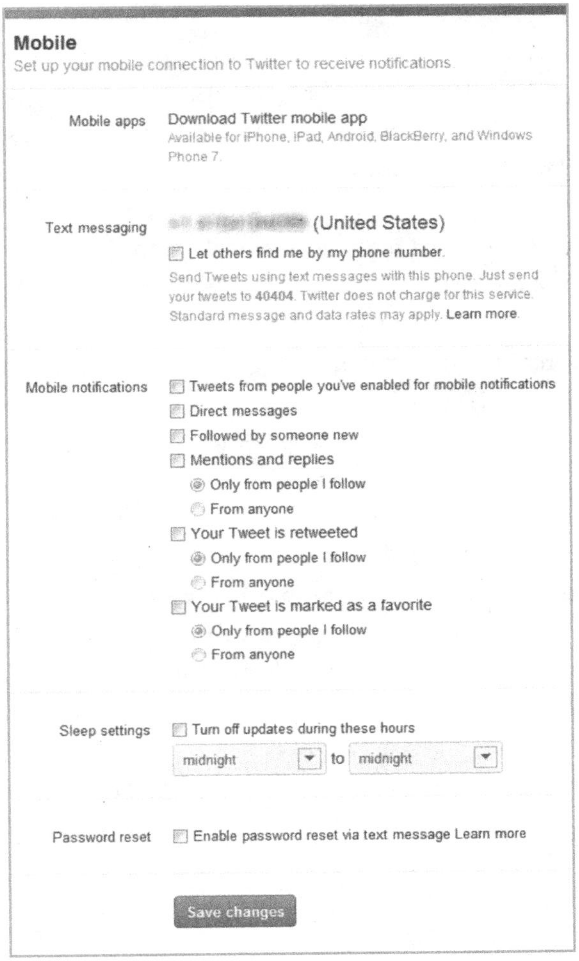

FIGURE 4–10. Notifications Options

Notifications

As I mentioned earlier, I don't like receiving a ton of messages from Twitter on my phone so I only enable the first option, *Tweets from people I've enabled for mobile notifications*. Occasionally, I will enable the *Direct message* option if I'm at a conference or event where people may be sending me direct messages when we're trying to find each other. Otherwise I leave the mobile notifications turned off and access Twitter through one of the apps on my phone.

Try enabling some of these notifications if you are just getting started on Twitter and building a following. Responding in a timely manner to Tweets, ReTweets, and Direct Messages is important when you are a small-business owner, so these notifications can be helpful. Large companies have teams of people monitoring and responding to Twitter activity. If you have a small team or are the only one responding to your company's Twitter activity, you should use these notifications.

Apple added native Twitter support to iOS 5 in October 2011 so you can seamlessly Tweet photos and Tweet directly from websites you're browsing with your iPhone, iPod, or iPad. Twitter app updates in early 2012 for Blackberry and Android users extended the same functionality to their mobile devices. Update your apps on a regular basis so you always have the latest and greatest features. Twitter is always enhancing their platform so you'll want to take full advantage of their new features.

The Notifications settings, shown in Figure 4–11, lets you configure your email notifications.

Receiving email notifications is a matter of personal preference. Some people want to receive an email for all Twitter activity, while others prefer not to be bothered. I find it very useful to receive email notifications when someone follows me or my Tweets are ReTweeted. I like to thank people personally when they follow me instead of using an automated program like www.socialoomph.com. You'll notice some Twitter users have an almost one-to-one follower to following ratio, meaning for every person who follows them, they automatically follow them back. Once they follow each other, an automated DM is sent thanking them for following them. Personally, I don't want to follow every

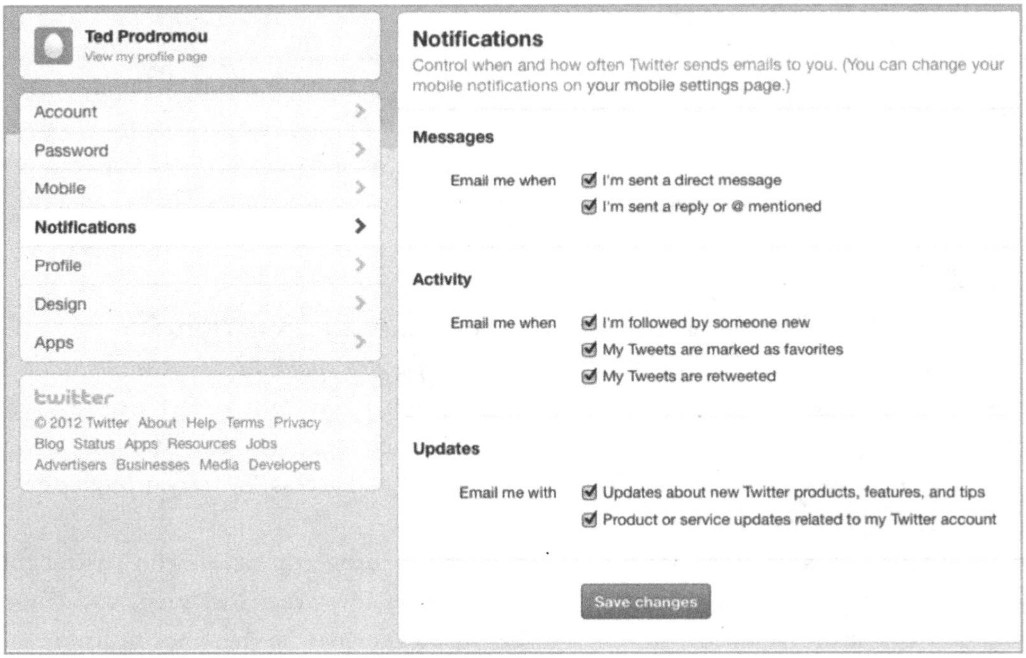

FIGURE 4–11. Let Twitter Know When to Notify You by Email

person who follows me (no offense, followers). I think I get more value by being selective in whom I follow, but that's my preference. Having 10,000 followers is more valuable to me than following 10,000 people.

Think about which email notifications you want to receive and which notifications will benefit you most. We all receive way too many emails every day, so adding Twitter notifications may not be worth your while. I think most people would benefit by receiving the emails sent in the Messages and Activity section shown in Figure 4–11 (page 54). Another option would be to set up a new Gmail or Yahoo! email address for your Twitter activity and set up a rule where the notifications automatically go into a folder. You can review the folder once a day or week so it won't clutter up your primary email inbox.

Profile

Let's move on to the next tab, Profile. As you see in Figure 4–12 shown on page 56, your default Twitter profile picture is an egg on a yellow background. If you don't upload a new profile picture, this is what people will see when they check your profile to decide whether to follow you. If I see the default Twitter egg on someone's profile, my first impression is that they aren't very interested in Twitter, so I probably won't get much value if I follow them. I've never seen anyone on Twitter using the default profile settings that Tweeted anything worthwhile on a consistent basis. I'm sure there are exceptions, but I don't need to waste my time following people with no profile picture. We talked about appropriate profile pictures earlier, so I won't get into that again. In brief, upload a friendly-looking headshot that isn't blurry or likely to offend the viewer.

I think it's a good idea to add your location to your Twitter profile to let people know where you are. You don't have to put your exact town if you are concerned about security. I live in the San Francisco Bay Area, so I put San Francisco as my location, not the suburb I live in. This lets people know approximately where I live so they can contact me if they also live in the area or if they are visiting. It's an easy way to create another bond between me and my followers.

Always add your website or blog URL in the Website section. Start your URL with http:// so it becomes a clickable link in your profile. If you start it with just *www*, then it won't become clickable. One trick is to set up a page on your blog or website where visitors can download a free report and use that URL in this section. That way, when followers visit your website or blog, you have an opportunity to capture their name and email address so you can build an email list of prospects. I've also seen scenarios where people put the URL of their blog or website in the Website box and add a link to a download page on their blog or website in their bio. For example, they would add

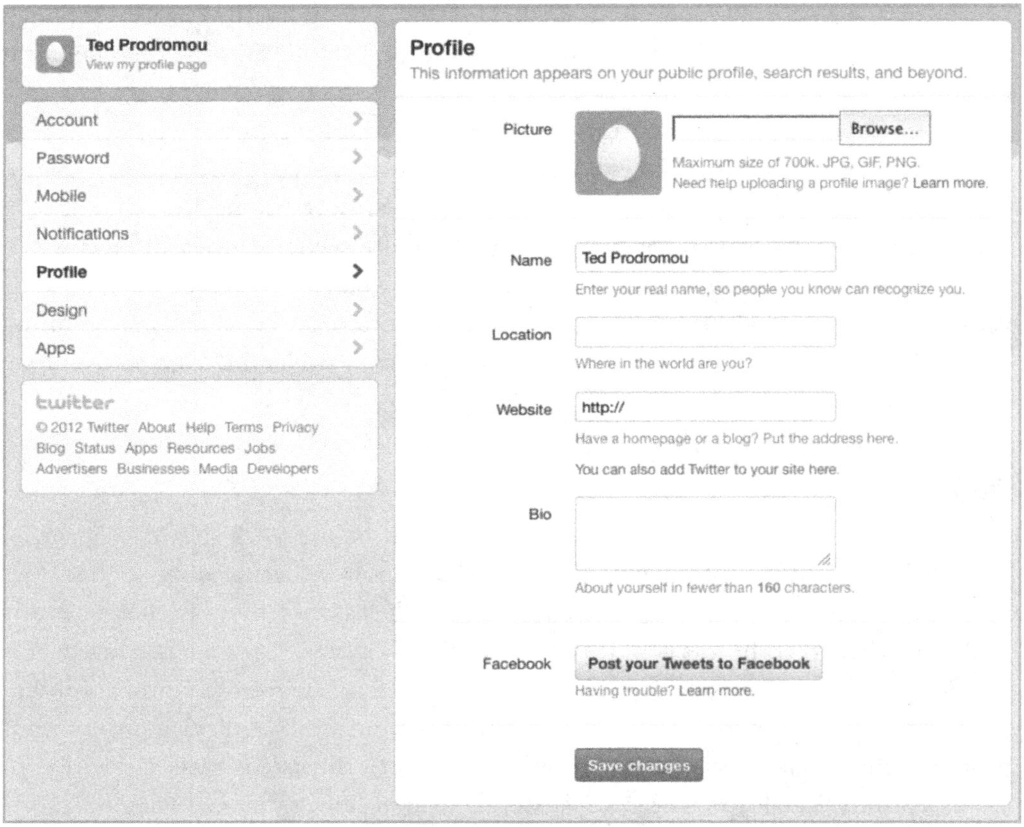

FIGURE 4–12. Your Twitter Profile Settings

http://website.com in the Website box and "Learn how to generate more leads at http://website.com/FreeReport" in their bio. It's a good trick to get you two links to your blog or website from a popular website that will help your search rankings.

We covered crafting your bio earlier so we won't get into detail again here. Use one of the approaches we described and create a bio that will grab people's attention. The more interesting your bio is, the more followers you will gain.

The last option is to connect your Twitter account with your Facebook account so your Tweets will automatically appear as Facebook status updates. I used to teach my students to connect all of their social media accounts together so they can post in one place and have it appear everywhere automatically. Today, I think it's better not to connect your social media accounts because something you Tweet may not be appropriate for your LinkedIn or Facebook status. My audience on Twitter is very different from my audience on LinkedIn. My Facebook friends are another completely different audience. Of course, there is some overlap in my connections across social communities, but for the most part they are connected with me on each social community for a reason. I speak very differently to my LinkedIn connections than I do with my Facebook friends. Now I create unique updates for each social media community. Sometimes I'm distributing the same free report, but I phrase my updates/posts differently for each audience. I find this much more effective than auto-blasting content to my different networks.

Design

The Design tab is where you customize your Twitter page with standard backgrounds that are included in your Twitter account or custom designed backgrounds. To get started, you can browse through the standard Twitter templates and select one you can use temporarily. In Figure 4–13 you see the standard Twitter backgrounds. You can also

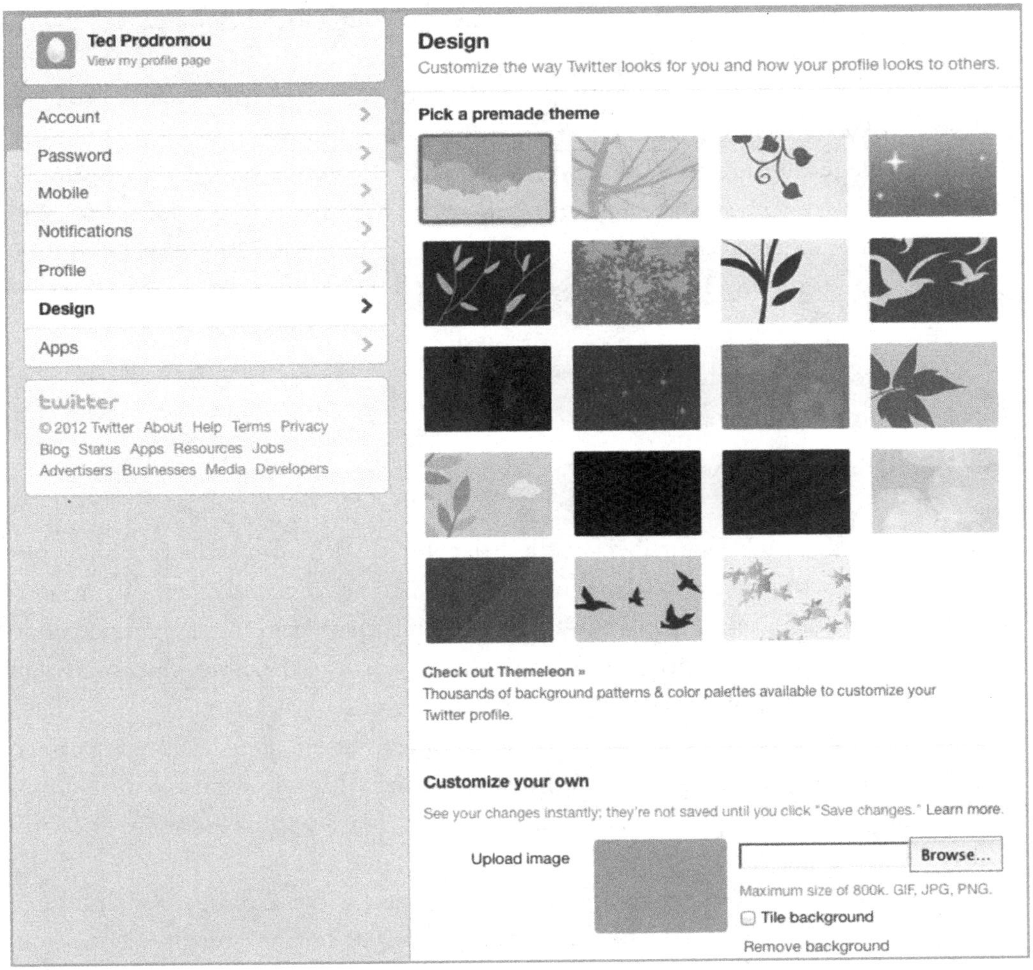

FIGURE 4–13. Selecting Your Generic-Twitter Background

Google "Twitter backgrounds" and find hundreds of free or cheap backgrounds you can upload to your Twitter page. I recommend creating your own custom background and uploading it to your Twitter page using the Customize Your Own option in the bottom right-hand corner as shown in Figure 4–13.

I see your Twitter page as an extension of your brand. Your social media pages should have the same look and feel as your website and blog. When people come to your website or blog, they become familiar with your logo and your company colors and fonts. When they come to your Twitter or Facebook page, they should see the same logo, colors, and fonts as they saw on your website and blog. It's Branding 101 and it's very easy to do.

Customizing Your Twitter Background

Because your Twitter homepage is an extension of your brand, it's important to create a custom background that contains your branding. Your Twitter homepage is divided into three columns. The middle column is your Twitter feed, which is 865 pixels wide and covers approximately half of the page. You can customize the small sidebars on either side of your Twitter feed. It's best to optimize your Twitter background for 1024 x 768 pixel wide resolutions so most of your visitors can view your Twitter page optimally. You can optimize your Twitter background for higher screen resolutions, but many visitors may not see your entire background.

I like to optimize my Twitter backgrounds as follows:

Left column:	66 pixels
Middle column (Twitter feed):	865 pixels
Right column:	66 pixels

Your background should be saved as a GIF, JPG, or PNG file and less than 800k in size.

You want to include your logo in the left column with your website and/or blog URLs so people can reach you. Also include your email address and telephone number. The key is to make it easy for people to contact you if they want more information about you or your company. Unfortunately, the sidebars are not clickable, so display your contact information prominently and make it easy to read.

Some Twitter homepages have additional information about the company or display products in the right column. Most companies leave images and text off the right column and just display the background image. Here are some examples of Twitter backgrounds from popular businesses.

Figure 4–14, page 59, shows the Twitter homepage for Zipcar. They choose to include images of their customers using Zipcar rentals. This is a great way to build customer loyalty. It gives their customers their "15 minutes of fame," as Andy Warhol

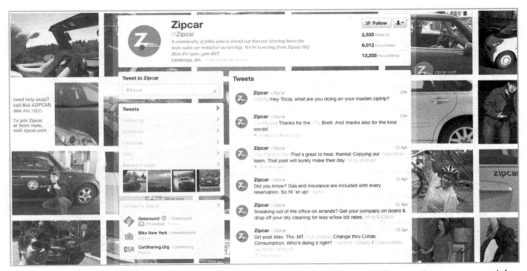

FIGURE 4–14. The Zipcar Twitter Homepage, Which Features Zipcar Customers with Their Rentals

used to say. Personally, I'm not a fan of this Twitter background because it's too busy for my taste, but it may appeal to you. Test different backgrounds and ask your followers for feedback. They'll definitely tell you what they think.

Spotify does a great job creating a background that matches their image and uses their green brand color. As you see in Figure 4–15, their background matches their hip image and their sidebar message is simple and makes it clear what they offer.

FIGURE 4–15. Spotify's Twitter Homepage Matches Their Branding Well

FIGURE 4–16. The Clean, Simple, and Traditional Look of Coca-Cola

Coca-Cola is a recognized brand worldwide and they use a very simple background image on their Twitter homepage. Figure 4–16 shows the traditional Coca-Cola red background with the water droplets you would see on a cold can of Coke. The traditional Coca-Cola logo is included just below their Twitter information in their feed.

SEOmoz does a great job using their branding in their Twitter background and makes it very easy to contact them. See the detailed contact information in the left sidebar in Figure 4–17 on page 61. Everything you need to know about SEOmoz is included in the left sidebar.

Don't reinvent the wheel. Look at other top brands and your competitors Twitter homepages and see what they're doing. Design your Twitter background so you incorporate what you like from their backgrounds and use your logo and brand colors. Keep your background clean and simple so your Twitter homepage looks professional and lets your prospects and customers easily contact you. If you don't have the skills to create your own Twitter background, you can have one created at www.fiverr.com for as little as $5 or you can create your own using a wizard at Themeleon at http://www. colourlovers.com/themeleon/twitter.

Let's move on to the next tab in your Twitter profile, the Applications, or Apps, tab.

Applications

The Applications tab is the last configuration tab in your Twitter profile. Figure 4–18 on page 61 shows you the App tab and which applications you've approved to interact with your Twitter account.

FIGURE 4–17. The SEOmoz Twitter Homepage with Detailed Contact Information in the Left Sidebar

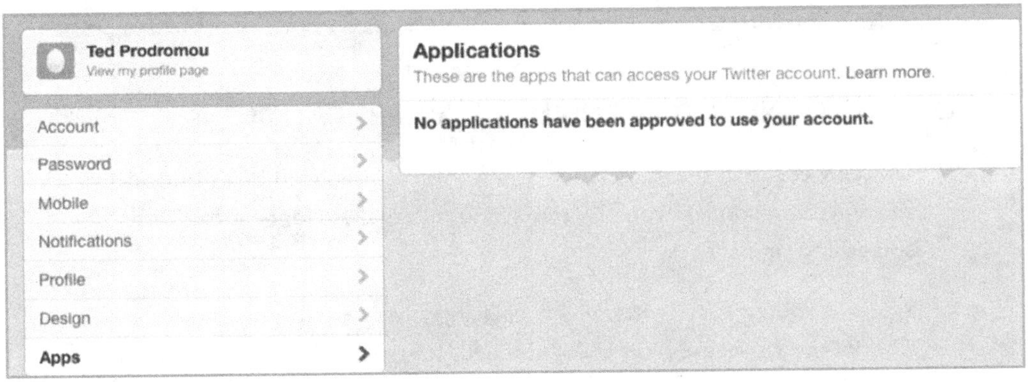

FIGURE 4–18. The Apps Tab Shows You Which Applications You Have Approved to Use Your Twitter Account

Here is what Twitter defines as an application that you may want to approve to work with your Twitter account:

Definition: A third-party application is a product created by a company other than Twitter and used to access Tweets and other Twitter data. For example, you can automatically share your Tweets on Facebook or instantaneously Tweet whenever you update your blog.

Connecting your Twitter account to third-party applications enhances your Twitter experience, making it easier to connect with more people and keep in touch with them. Some of the more popular applications you may want to add to your Twitter account include:

- Twitpic (www.twitpic.com): Photo sharing tool for Twitter
- Bit.ly (www.bitly.com): URL shortener
- Yfrog (www.yfrog.com): Photo video sharing tool for Twitter
- HootSuite (www.hootsuite.com): Browser-based social media client
- TweetMeme www.tweetmeme.com: Twitter ReTweet directory
- Adf.ly (www.adf.ly): URL shortener with advertising
- TinyURL (http://tinyurl.com): URL shortener
- Paper.li (http://paper.li): Tweet digests
- Goo.gl (http://goo.gl/): Google's URL shortener
- Topsy (http://topsy.com): Twitter search engine
- TwitterFeed (http://twitterfeed.com): RSS to Twitter and Facebook automation tool
- Ow.ly (http://ow.ly/url/shorten-url): HootSuite's URL shortener
- TwitCause (https://twitter.com/TwitCause): Help support causes (from the Experience Project)

HOW TO CONNECT TO A THIRD-PARTY APPLICATION

1. On the website of the application you want to connect, find the button/link asking you to connect your Twitter account (usually "Connect to Twitter" or something similar).

2. You'll be routed to a Twitter website asking you to log in to your account. Check that it's secure by verifying the URL starts with https://twitter.com.

3. After logging in, Twitter will ask you to approve the application.

4. Be sure to review the various permissions you are granting to the application. These are listed in green (what the app can do with your account) and red (what the app can't do).

5. Click *Authorize app* if you'd like to connect.

You're now connected! Review your authorized applications to remove/revoke access anytime.

- Social Oomph (www.socialoomph.com): Twitter automation and management tool
- Twitter Counter (http://twittercounter.com): Twitter profile statistics
- TweetDeck (https://twitter.com/TweetDeck): Browser-based social media client (note that their PC client is more popular but does not show up as a website visit)
- Mobypicture (www.mobypicture.com): Photo, video, audio and text sharing in social media tool
- Favstar.fm (http://favstar.fm): Analyze Tweets by number of Favorites and ReTweets
- Sponsored Tweets (http://sponsoredtweets.com): Twitter advertising
- Friend or Follow? (http://friendorfollow.com): Follower management tool
- WeFollow (http://wefollow.com): Twitter user directory
- Social Mention (http://socialmention.com): Social media search engine
- Seesmic (http://seesmic.com): Browser-based social media client
- CoTweet (http://cotweet.com): Browser-based social media client

There are hundreds of other Twitter applications, with more being developed every day as Twitter gains popularity. We'll cover Twitter applications in more detail in Chapter 8.

You can also download apps directly from the Apple App Store or the Android App Collections and the app will prompt you through the authorization process as you are installing it. If you remove an app from your phone, don't forget to revoke access to the app in your Twitter account.

THE @ CONNECT TAB

You would think the @ Connect tab would be where you would find like-minded people to follow, but it's more about showing you a snapshot of your Twitter activity. The @ Connect tab is where you see your Twitter interactions and when people have mentioned you. It's not about connecting at all unless you want to start following some celebrities.

Figure 4–19 on page 63 shows you the two tabs on the Connect page. First you see Interactions, which, when you click on it, shows your Tweets, mentions of you by others, new people you are following, as well as those who recently followed you. Twitter also recommends who to follow here, but it usually just recommends celebrities until you are following some of your colleagues and friends. The Twitter algorithm will recommend people to follow based on what keywords you put in your bio and where you live.

The next subsection is Mentions, where you will see a list of Tweets from other people who have mentioned your Twitter name in a Tweet. Because you're just getting started on Twitter you won't see any mentions until you have some followers who Tweet about you. See Figure 4–20 on page 63 to see the Mentions page.

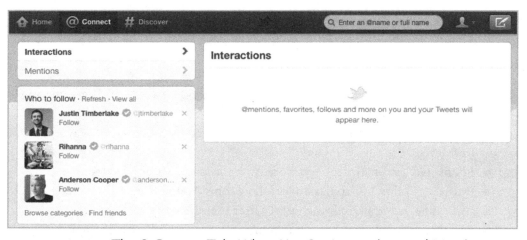

FIGURE 4–19. The @ Connect Tab, Where You See Interactions and Mentions

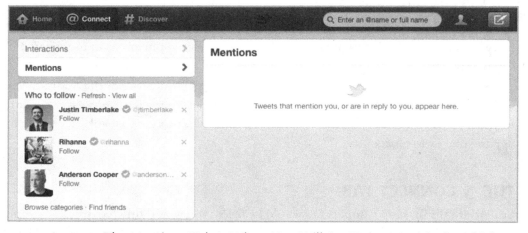

FIGURE 4–20. The Mentions Tab Is Where You Will See Twitter Activity in Which Someone Includes Your Twitter Name in a Tweet

For example, let's say I want to reach out to Chris Brogan on Twitter and send him a link to an interesting article. I'll create a Tweet that looks like this: "@chrisbrogan check out this great article that mentions your new website" and include a link to the article in the Tweet.

I could also mention one of Chris's blog posts in a Tweet by Tweeting, "I just read a great blog post about customer engagement by @chrisbrogan" and include a link to his blog post.

Both of these Tweets would show up in Chris Brogan's Twitter account under Mentions. I'll talk about writing interesting and interactive Tweets a bit later in the book. For now, let's get back to exploring the options available in your Twitter account.

Now that your Twitter profile is fully configured, including your custom background and an inviting bio and profile picture, you can start connecting with others.

CONCLUSION

Your Twitter profile is now taking shape. Continue experimenting with your Twitter bio and keywords to see which generate the best results for you.

In the next chapter, I'll show you how to create a comprehensive Twitter strategy so you can get the most from Twitter with minimal effort.

Following and Followers— the Foundation of Your Twitter Strategy

Twitter is almost useless if you don't follow people and others don't follow you. You can watch Twitter Trends and see what people are Tweeting about, but you won't see anything in your Mentions or Interactions tabs. It's like not having any friends in real life to hang out with and share your thoughts. We need conversation and engagement to make our lives more interesting and our businesses more successful. Following others on Twitter is a great way to start those conversations. Once you start following others and engaging in conversations, others will start to follow you.

THE ART OF FOLLOWING

Now you see why I wanted you to be patient before you started following people and Tweeting. At first glance, it looks like setting up your Twitter account is quick and easy. If you're using Twitter for fun, you can be up and Tweeting in a couple of minutes. Because you are using Twitter to promote your business and/or your personal brand, you needed to build your Twitter foundation before you jumped into the Twitterverse.

It's time to start following some interesting people so you can observe how they use Twitter. There are many ways to use Twitter, so you want to spend some time observing others to see which style works best for you.

TWITTER STYLES

Here are some Twitter styles you'll see as you explore the Twitterverse. I recommend choosing a style and sticking to it. If you want to combine styles, you may want to set up separate Twitter accounts so you don't confuse or alienate your followers. People will follow you because they like the information you provide in a particular style. If they follow you because they like your wit and wisdom and then you start auto-Tweeting content every few minutes in between your personal Tweets, you will overwhelm them and run the risk that they will unfollow you.

Let's explore some different Twitter styles so you can see which one fits your business.

The Screener

This person shares useful content with his or her followers and also ReTweets great Tweets from the people they follow. They are good listeners and are careful to share information that is relevant to the people they Tweet with every day.

The Thought Leader

This person targets a particular industry or niche. They Tweet relevant information based on the industry or niche. They are well respected in their particular field and their opinion is highly valued by the people who follow them.

The Linker

This person Tweets links to blog posts and/or affiliate links on their stream. They're probably using a Twitter tool to automatically Tweet RSS feeds from popular blogs or links from their blog that contain affiliate links. They rarely engage anyone in conversation.

The Reciprocator

Volume is their goal. They will often Tweet someone and tell them to follow them and will reciprocate by following them back. They often use automated tools to automatically follow everyone who follows them. You can spot them by looking at their profile and seeing an almost equal number of followers and following. They usually follow well over 10,000 people and have just as many following them.

The Trendsetter

These are usually celebrities or well-known personalities. Lady Gaga, Kim Kardashian, and sports figures are among this group. People watch for their Tweets, and celebrities are often compensated for their Tweets by sponsors.

The Matchmaker

This person spends a lot of time "listening" on Twitter and connecting people with like interests. We all know these people in our offline life. They love to connect people with like interests and are doing the same on Twitter.

The Chatterbox

They engage with others constantly. They rarely Tweet links to information. They love personal interaction online and offline. These are the same people who talk your ear off at parties and networking events.

The ReTweeter

This person spends most of their time ReTweeting other people's Tweets. They rarely share links they find on their own. They are masters of the ReTweet.

The Twitter-holic

These people Tweet like their lives depend on it. They're often accused of sharing TMI, too much information. They Tweet about their pet peeves, what they're wearing, what their neighbor is wearing, every craving they have, their sex life (or lack thereof) and everything else you didn't want to know about them. Every thought that crosses their mind is transformed into a Tweet. They Tweet at least 20 times every hour they are awake and may Tweet over 10,000 times a month. They don't need automated Tweets because there is no room on their Twitter feed for more Tweets. These people have a very high unfollow rate.

Of course, you will see hybrids of these styles, which can be confusing if you are following someone. As I mentioned earlier, I recommend choosing one of these styles and sticking to it as much as you can. Of course, you can deviate occasionally, but it's best to focus on one primary style.

As you come across these styles on Twitter, follow the person for a while so you get a sense of how they're using Twitter. Notice if they have a lot of followers and engagement with others. You are Tweeting to generate business, so I recommend choosing a style like The Screener or The Thought Leader. This way you will be sharing great information with others and engaging with them, enhancing your Twitter reputation.

Once you choose your Twitter style, you will want to start following other Twitter users who use the same style and in your industry or niche. Conversations will naturally occur because you are all using the same style and speak a common language related to your niche. It's no different than in your offline life. You have hobbies and interests that connect you with different circles of friends. If you are interested in softball, you join a team, creating a circle of friends related to softball. If you are interested in quilting, you may join a quilting club in your hometown. Once you join that circle, you have a common language related to that hobby and you have an instant connection.

FINDING THE RIGHT PEOPLE TO FOLLOW

So how do you find these people on Twitter? As you see in Figure 5-1, the # Discover tab helps you find people to follow using a variety of methods.

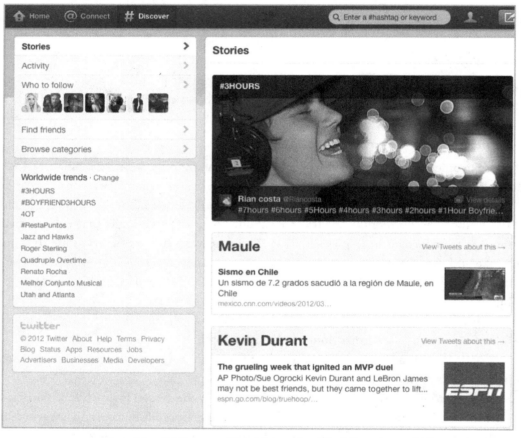

FIGURE 5-1. The # Discover Tab Helps You Find People to Follow

Finding People to Follow from Stories

When you click on the Stories tab under # Discover, Twitter will display a list of current news stories or popular Twitter topics so you can see who's Tweeting about that story. This is an easy way to attract attention to your Tweets. You add your take on the current event in your Tweet and leverage their Twitter popularity by Mentioning them or Replying to their Tweets. When you do this, your Tweet will be associated with the current news event and the person who originally Tweeted about it. Your Tweet may appear in the Stories tab and will appear in the Twitter stream of everyone who is following the hashtag of the current event and the people who are following the original Tweeter.

The # Discover Activity Tab

The # Discover Activity tab will display the Twitter activity of the people or companies you follow. As you see in Figure 5–2, this tab will introduce you to many new people who are connected to the people you follow. This is a great way to expand your circle of influence on Twitter and grow your Twitter network in a very targeted way.

The # Discover Who to Follow tab

The next tab is the Who to Follow tab, which contains recommendations from Twitter based on their proprietary algorithm. The Twitter algorithm reads all Twitter profiles

FIGURE 5–2. The # Discover Activity Section Shows the Activity of the People You Follow

and matches you up with people who have similar keywords in their profiles, work in the same industry, or are connected to people you follow. Figure 5–3 shows you some people Twitter recommended I follow based on similarities in our profiles or in the people we follow.

FIGURE 5–3. The Who To Follow Tab Recommends People Who Have Something in Common with You

The # Discover Find Friends Tab

The Find Friends tab lets you search for Twitter hashtags or keywords so you can find people to follow. If you are looking for your friends or specific companies on Twitter, just enter their name in the Search box to search Twitter's database. This function is also called Twitter Search and works exactly like Google or any other search engine. Figure 5–4 on page 73 shows you the Find Friends tab.

The other function of the Find Friends tab is to let you import your email contact databases into Twitter so you can send automated emails to your existing contacts. I do not recommend importing your email contacts into Twitter. When you import your email contacts into Twitter, the system automatically sends them a canned message that you can't personalize. It's very impersonal and is almost like spamming your

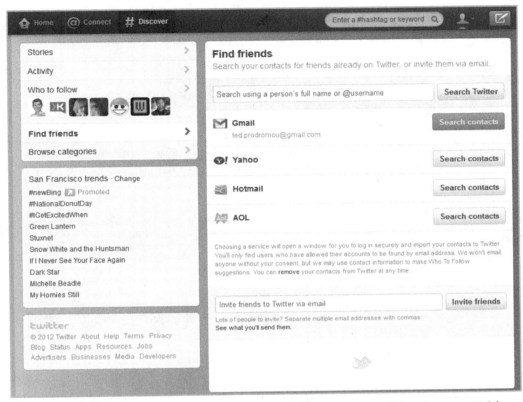

FIGURE 5–4. The Find Friends Tab Helps You Find More People to Connect With

email contacts. Instead of automatically inviting your contacts to join you on Twitter, I recommend connecting with them one at a time by following them, and then send them a personal email inviting them to follow you on Twitter. I feel this is a more personal approach that will enhance your relationship instead of sending them an automated message.

The # Discover Browse Categories Tab

Twitter has so much content, people were starting to have trouble finding what and who they were looking for. Most major companies, celebrities, musicians, and athletes are on Twitter but it was hard to find them because many don't use their names as their Twitter handle. For example, Ashton Kutcher uses @aplusk as his Twitter handle instead of @ ashtonkutcher. If you wanted to follow him it might be hard to find him in a Twitter Search. By searching the Entertainment category, you can narrow your search and easily find who you are looking for. Figure 5–5 on page 74 shows you the Browse Categories tab.

FIGURE 5–5. The Browse Categories Tab Segments Twitter Content into Easy-to-Navigate Categories

BUILDING YOUR FOLLOWERS

Most people think they don't have control of who follows them. When I was starting out on Twitter, I didn't think I could control who followed me, but my personal experience proved me wrong. I've learned not to assume anything when it comes to social media, and Twitter is no exception.

When I first signed up for Twitter, I was pretty active, Tweeting a few times a day, engaging in conversations, and following others. After a few months, I took a break from Twitter and noticed my number of new followers slowed and eventually stopped. When I started Tweeting again and engaging with others, people started following me again. There seemed to be a direct correlation. The more I Tweeted and followed others, the more people followed me. I was pretty excited when I discovered this simple trick!

My experience on Twitter was very similar to attending an in-person networking event. When you attend a networking event and you are actively engaging with others, people take notice and approach you. When you stand off to the side and don't participate in conversations, people tend to ignore you.

When I was active on Twitter, people started following me. When I was inactive on Twitter, people ignored me. I also noticed that the people following me were in the same niche as the people I was engaging with. When I engaged with online marketers, people interested in online marketing followed me. When I engaged with people about family-related topics, people interested in family-related topics followed me.

This simple exercise taught me that building your followers on Twitter is actually very easy. The Twitter algorithm does a great job suggesting people to follow based on your Twitter patterns. The algorithm looks at the keywords in Twitter user profiles and in your Tweets to match Twitter users. This is why it is important to use keywords in your Twitter profile, your Tweets, and your hashtags so Twitter will match you up with your target audience.

CONCLUSION

You now have a solid understanding of whom you want to follow on Twitter and why you should be following them. You also know the different styles of Twitter users so you'll be able to recognize them when they follow you or when you are deciding whether to follow someone. Building your Twitter network is similar to building your business network on LinkedIn. You want to follow the right people so you won't overwhelm your Twitterstream with useless Tweets from people who won't provide value to your business network.

In the next chapter, you're going to learn how to align your Twitter strategy with your business so Twitter can become an effective marketing channel to spread the word about your products and services.

Chapter 6

Aligning Your Twitter Strategy with Your Business

There are many ways to use Twitter, but you want to use it in the most efficient, effective way to grow your business. Like all social media sites, you can easily get lost and waste a lot of time on Twitter. You see an interesting Tweet, click on a link, download an interesting white paper, and the next thing you know it's two hours later. When you create and execute a comprehensive Twitter strategy for your business, your wasted time will be minimized.

It can be easy to get frustrated with Twitter if you don't take the time to create a strategy. Twitter is another marketing channel for promoting your business, so you need to extend your marketing strategy to include it with other social media sites. Every Tweet you do should have a very specific purpose, whether it's to promote a new white paper or announce a new webinar. Every person or company you follow should be followed for a reason. Your Twitter activity should be part of a bigger marketing campaign. When you take the time to create a comprehensive Twitter strategy, you will see dramatic results.

TWITTER STRATEGIES

Most small businesses use only one Twitter account for their business, which makes perfect sense. Your Twitter account name should be your business or brand name. Some companies dedicate one person to do their Tweeting while others have multiple people sharing the account. I'll discuss each scenario to show you the best practices for each approach.

Whether you have one person Tweeting or a team managing your Twitter account, here are some Twitter best practices for account management.

- Tweet at least 10 to 20 times per day. You should schedule four to six Tweets per day that include links to content on your website or promote your company events such as workshops, webinars, or training classes. You should engage with your Twitter Followers at least four to six times per day and the rest of the Tweets should be ReTweets or Mentions of other Tweets related to your company, products, or your industry.
- Especially if you have a team managing your Twitter account, try to maintain a consistent voice in your Tweets so people will not be able to tell that you have multiple people doing your Tweeting.
- Use tools like Hootsuite that provide analytics so you can measure your Twitter activity. Create reports that show which Tweets receive the most ReTweets and Mentions. Also monitor your click activity to see which Tweets and content are most popular.
- Use tools like Hootsuite that have the ability to manage workflow. In Chapter 8 I'll get into more detail about the Twitter monitoring tools that let you manage workflow. This lets you assign Tweets to specific team members who have the

---

TWITTER IN YOUR BUSINESS

Your Twitter strategy needs to be in alignment with your business strategy. You can use Twitter for many business reasons:

- As a marketing channel, Twitter can be used to build your brand and generate leads.

- To generate sales

- To provide technical and/or customer support

- To manage your company's reputation

---

appropriate expertise. This also prevents duplicate Tweets coming from your accounts. You have a complete history of your Tweets and responses so you know exactly which team member did the Tweeting.

CREATE A TWITTER PLAN FOR MARKETING, SALES, SUPPORT, AND REPUTATION MANAGEMENT

Businesses are discovering that Twitter is a very effective tool for marketing, sales, technical support, and customer support. Your prospects and customers are talking about you and your competitors on Twitter, so you need to be listening to what they say and adapting your Twitter strategy to respond to their conversations. You can also use Twitter to proactively promote your brand, generate leads, promote company events and engage with your customers and prospects in real time. Let's see how you can use Twitter throughout your company.

Marketing

Businesses are effectively using Twitter for inbound and outbound marketing. Here are some ideas for using Twitter as a marketing channel.

- *Promote your brand by optimizing your Twitter profile.* Be sure to:
  - Use your logo as your profile picture
  - Use your brand name as your Twitter handle and your Twitter username
  - Use your brand name in your Twitter bio and add a link to a white paper in your bio
  - Add your website URL to your profile
  - Use your brand name as your hashtag and include it in all Tweets

- *Generate leads* by offering white papers, instructional videos, e-books, and product samples if appropriate. Write a compelling Tweet with a link to the lead gen asset.
  - Always send visitors to a separate landing page with an opt-in form for each asset you Tweeted about. See Figure 6–1 on page 80 to see a sample landing page with an opt-in web form.
  - After visitors opt in to receive the asset, follow up with a series of emails that introduce them to your products and to additional white papers, videos, and e-books.
  - Track your results so you know which assets are most popular and which Tweets generate the best response. Tweets are like subject lines in your emails, so track your Tweets in a spreadsheet so you know which work best.

FIGURE 6–1. A Landing Page with an Opt-In Web Form

- *Promote webinars, conferences, training classes and other events sponsored by your company.* Write Tweets that promote the events and include a link to a landing page where they can sign up for the events. Again, use a separate landing page for each event and track your results.

- *Promote your brand using Twitter advertising.* We will get into Twitter advertising in the section "Twitter Promoted Services" beginning on page 87.

- *Display the Twitter logo prominently on your website and encourage people to Follow you on Twitter.* Also add links to your Twitter page in your email footer, on your blogs, and in your email newsletters. Constantly ask people to Follow you in all of your marketing materials.

■ *If appropriate, you can offer discount codes in your Tweets.*

The key to success when using Twitter for marketing is to carefully plan your Twitter marketing campaigns and measure your results so you can replicate the campaigns that work.

Sales

Twitter has become a very effective sales tool for both B2B and B2C businesses. In B2B sales, Twitter helps you keep your name in front of prospects when you have a long sales cycle. In B2C sales, you can Tweet promotions and coupon codes, and create contests to generate sales. Here are some ideas for using Twitter for sales.

■ *Listen!* Monitor your competitors' brand names and hashtags to see what people are saying about them on Twitter. When you see negative Tweets about their products or service, use it as a competitive selling point. Listen for positive and negative comments about your products and services, as well. Engage unsatisfied customers or prospects immediately to defuse the situation. The key is to address their concerns quickly so you can turn the negative sentiment into positive sentiment publicly.

■ *Use Twitter Search to find people using your target keywords in their Twitter profiles, hashtags, and Tweets.* They may be dissatisfied with your competitor's product and are looking for a solution to their problem. These people are potential prospects, so you should check out their profiles and Follow them. After you Follow them, see who they are Following and keep Following more potential prospects as you find them. Add your prospects to a Twitter list so it's easier for you to monitor and communicate with them.

■ *When you have a prospect in your sales funnel, engage them in conversation publicly on Twitter.* Send them links to new white papers or videos to introduce them to new features in your products.

■ *Hold contests to generate sales.* You could have people Tweet a picture of themselves using your product, with the winner receiving a discount on their next purchase.

■ *Tweet coupon codes.* One of the most popular searches on Twitter Search is for "coupon codes" for specific brands or products.

There are plenty of other ways to use Twitter for sales. Think of Twitter as another communication channel and listen to what people are telling you. You will be surprised at what people are Tweeting about and they'll be grateful when you reach out to them.

Support

When you monitor Twitter for your brand name or the names of your products, you will see a lot of people asking questions or asking for assistance. People expect you to respond to them when they Tweet for help. People will ask for help on Twitter even though it may not be your formal support channel. The good news is that many times, other people who don't work for your company will answer their question. This is very common in the tech industry.

Comcast made Twitter support famous when they started @comcastcares and monitored for the keyword Comcast. People were complaining about problems with their Comcast products or waiting for a technician to arrive who was late. Frank Eliason, a former Comcast employee, started the @comcastcares Twitter account and responded to customer Tweets for help. He resolved many issues via Twitter and dispatched technicians when he couldn't. He instantly turned many angry Comcast customers into raving fans by responding to their Tweets. How can you use Twitter to enhance your customer support?

- *Listen!* Monitor Twitter for your brand name and product names. Identify the products or services that receive support requests via Twitter. Designate specific people with the right expertise to respond to those questions in a timely manner.

- *Create specific Twitter accounts or hashtags for each product* so the correct technician can respond to the questions. Computer Associates has over 20 Twitter accounts, each one for a specific product.

- *Tweet product updates* to let your customers know a new version is available.

- *Tweet when your service is down* or having problems. If you are a utility company, you can Tweet service update messages during and after storms.

People are reaching out to your company for help whether you know it or not. You can't ignore it or the problem will turn into a PR nightmare. Be proactive and respond to their Tweets for help in a timely manner, and your customers will love you.

Reputation Management

The internet and social media has provided a new communication channel for customers to complain about defective products or shoddy service. We've all heard that a dissatisfied customer will tell 20 friends about their bad experience but a satisfied customer won't tell anyone. Today, the internet lets dissatisfied customers tell *millions* of people around the world that they are unhappy with your product in seconds. If you try to ignore it, the problem only gets worse.

Social media, including Twitter, lets you address negative events quickly and very publicly. When something bad happens to your company, news travels very fast, so you need to be ready to respond quickly and professionally. Here are some tips to avoid PR nightmares and protect your company's reputation.

- *Use tools to monitor all social media* communication channels for negative events.

- *Have a plan* ready in advance in case a negative event happens. Create a response team in advance. This team will immediately discuss negative events, determine the best response, and respond as fast as possible on all social media channels.

- *Use Twitter to proactively* announce new products and company news items. Tweet a link to a landing page, not to the homepage of your website, so people can easily read the news you are promoting.

- *Use Twitter to promote press releases* that announce company events and awards you've won. Tweet your own horn!

Social media is a double-edged sword. It's a very powerful tool that can hurt you as much as it can help you. You need to be proactive and monitor your brand name and keywords 24/7 and respond quickly to requests. Address negative sentiment immediately to limit the damage. The key is to respond quickly in a positive, helpful way.

CHOOSE THE AUDIENCE YOU WANT TO REACH

With over 150 million users on Twitter, you can reach just about any audience you want. Many Twitter users are using it just for fun and aren't interested in what you have to sell, at least while they're using Twitter. You need to focus on your demographic so you're sending your message to the right audience and connecting with the right people. You don't want to try to sell ice to Eskimos in the middle of winter.

Once you identify your audience, start searching for their company names or keywords. When you find some prospects, see whom they're communicating with and what they're talking about. Look for common themes and threads so you can join the discussion. As you find potential prospects, Follow them and add them to a Twitter List so it's easier to monitor their activity.

For example, say you were attending the Microsoft Worldwide Partner Conference and you wanted to connect with other attendees. You can do a Twitter Search for the conference hashtag, #WPC. There'll be conversations related to the conference as you see in Figure 6–2 on page 84. You can easily connect with other conference attendees and see what the hot conference topics are.

FIGURE 6–2. A Twitter Search for #WPC Shows Conversations Related to the Microsoft Worldwide Partner Conference

SPEAK YOUR AUDIENCE'S LANGUAGE, WHETHER IT'S TECH TALK, MARKETING TALK, OR SALES TALK

After Following your prospects, you will learn what they are talking about on Twitter and how they are saying it. They'll use slang and industry acronyms as well as some terms that may not be familiar to you. Notice what they're saying and how they are saying it so you can jump into their Twitter conversations and fit right in. If you reach out to a prospect on Twitter and try to engage them using old terminology or the wrong slang, they will be less likely to connect with you. Twitter and social media have their own language, so "listen" awhile until you get the hang of this new language. Make sure you use the same hashtags and abbreviations your prospects are using when you want to jump into the conversation.

Imagine you are at a networking event or cocktail party and you want to join a conversation that is already in progress. You wouldn't interrupt and steer the conversation in a different direction. You would listen politely and add value so they would welcome you into the conversation. If you jump in aggressively and start talking about something totally different than they're talking about, you may offend them and the conversation will end abruptly, ending your chances of getting to know them better. On Twitter, just as you would at in-person networking events, it's always best to listen at least 80 percent of the time and speak only when you can add value to the conversation.

TRACK YOUR TWITTER ACTIVITY AND MEASURE ENGAGEMENT

There are plenty of social media monitoring tools ranging from free to very expensive. You'll learn more about Twitter Tools in Chapter 8, but for now just know that you will need to start using some tools to measure your level of engagement on Twitter. Some of the Twitter activities you will need to monitor include:

- Number of Tweets
- Number of Followers
- Number of people you are Following
- Number of ReTweets
- Number of Mentions
- Number of Replies
- Sentiment, which is a measurement of social media comments with respect to a positive or negative tone
- Twitter visitor-to-lead ratio

Most social media monitoring tools will provide this data for you. Measuring your Twitter activity will tell you what your customers and prospects are interested in, what they think of your brand and products, what they think of the content you're Tweeting, and the overall sentiment of your Twitter activity.

Your goal is to engage your prospects and customers on Twitter, have them click on the links in your Tweets, ReTweet your Tweets, and Mention you and your brand as often as possible. You are trying to create a buzz about your brand on Twitter that will have a viral effect that spreads to other social media sites and throughout the internet. You can measure the viral effect of your Tweets and the performance of your Twitter marketing campaigns by carefully planning and measuring every Tweet.

TRACK YOUR LEAD-GENERATION EFFORTS

You should always measure your marketing campaigns and lead-generation efforts. Twitter and other social media websites are just tools to get your message out, and a small part of the overall marketing campaign. Of course, you want to measure your Twitter activity, but you also want to measure the effectiveness of your overall marketing campaign. Some of the factors you want to measure in your marketing campaigns include:

- How many times did they click on the links in my campaign?
- How many times did they fill out the opt-in form? This is your conversion rate, the number of clicks divided by the number of people who filled out the form.
- How many people opened the follow-up email?
- How many completed your call to action from the follow-up email?
- How many people became customers from the marketing campaign?
- How long did they remain customers?
- What is the lifetime value of a customer? This is the total amount of money you made from each customer while they remained your customer.
- What was your cost per lead for the marketing campaign?

As you see, it's more than just measuring how many people ReTweeted your Tweets or clicked on your links. You need to look at the big picture and see which marketing campaigns are most effective in turning prospects into customers. Once they are customers, you need to keep marketing and nurturing them to keep them customers for as long as possible.

MONITOR YOUR REPUTATION

Reputation management has been around forever but has taken on a new meaning since the evolution of social media and the internet, where bad news travels very fast. You have to proactively monitor your brand so you can respond quickly to negative events. Many times in the past, poor handling of negative events has nearly destroyed many companies.

In 2011, Research in Motion, RIM, who manufactures the BlackBerry smartphone, had many service issues where messages were not being delivered and they experienced many network-wide service outages. Instead of proactively announcing they had service issues, they chose not to let their customers know that their messages weren't being delivered to Europe. The problem lasted for days and the problem spread throughout their network. BlackBerry users were outraged that RIM was denying or not acknowledging a problem. Eventually, BlackBerry users took to Twitter to complain, and the backlash was tremendous. Because RIM chose to not let its customers know there was a problem, its reputation was permanently damaged and the company has suffered a significant loss of standing in a market they used to dominate.

ASSIGN DUTIES TO THE APPROPRIATE DEPARTMENTS

If you have multiple products that require specific expertise to support, you should have separate Twitter accounts for each product. If you have specialists for each product on your help desk they should be monitoring Twitter for their product so they can respond with appropriate answers. Figure 6–3 on page 88 shows the Twitter accounts for Cisco.

As you see, Cisco has many Twitter accounts so customers can easily connect with the right solution provider. If they only had one Twitter account, their Tweet stream would be too active to be useful because there would be so many unrelated Tweets. Using separate Twitter accounts for each product and service, Cisco can provide a higher level of support to its customers.

Maybe your company isn't as large as Cisco but you may want to consider using multiple Twitter accounts so you can provide better customer service.

TWITTER-PROMOTED SERVICES

For years, Twitter provided its service for free and they didn't have a way to generate revenue. Of course, no business can provide a service for free without eventually going out of business. We knew Twitter would eventually have to offer advertising or a way to generate revenue, and we're starting to see some paid services from Twitter.

Promoted Accounts

This service lets you promote your Twitter account to increase your brand exposure. When you use Promoted Accounts, your Twitter account will be featured in search results and within the Who To Follow section. You learned about Who To Follow in Chapter 2 and how it identifies similar accounts and followers to help you discover new businesses, content, and people on Twitter. Your Promoted Account appears in the Who To Follow section for users who have been identified as most likely to have interests similar to you.

I like to use Promoted Accounts when we are about to launch a new product or make a significant announcement about our company. Getting our Twitter account in front of millions of targeted Twitter users exponentially increases the reach of our announcement.

Promoted Tweets

Promoted Tweets is similar to the Promoted Accounts service but you're promoting a specific Tweet instead of promoting your Twitter account. A Promoted Tweet is like a

FIGURE 6–3. Cisco Has Numerous Twitter Accounts to Provide Specialized Support for Each Product and Service

Google ad where you're trying to get people to click on the link in the ad so they can take further action.

Promoted Tweets that engage and resonate with users are more likely to appear so it's important to use Tweets you know receive a good response. You can do this testing in advance by creating a series of Tweets with different messages and landing pages so you know which one converts best. You want to use a Tweet that not only receives a lot of clicks but also receives a lot of conversions on your landing page.

Promoted Tweets appear in many targeted locations on Twitter. They appear in search, timelines, targeted followers, and on both mobile and desktop devices.

- *Promoted Tweets in search*: Your Promoted Tweets will appear at the top of the results page when people do Twitter searches based on the keywords you target.
- *Promoted Tweets in timelines*: Promoted Tweets can be targeted to users' timelines who are similar to your followers. This lets you get your message in front of people who are just like your current Twitter network and will be more receptive to your message.
- *Targeting across mobile and desktop*: You can target your Promoted Tweets to desktop or mobile devices. This lets you target buyers who are more likely to purchase your products or respond to your marketing message.
- *Geographic targeting*: Promoted Tweets can be targeted to specific countries or to specific regions in the U.S. This lets you create targeted messages for each country or region that will convert better than broad marketing messages.

You only pay when someone ReTweets, replies to, clicks, or favorites your Promoted Tweet, and impressions on ReTweets are free. This extends the reach of your campaigns, significantly.

I like to use Promoted Tweets for lead generation and to promote new products. Since Promoted Tweets appear in different areas of Twitter, it's okay to run them at the same time you are running a Promoted Accounts campaign. This gives you maximum exposure for your new product announcement.

Don't overdo Promoted Tweets. I like to rotate the Promoted Tweet campaigns and target them to different keyword phrases so your ads aren't seen so often that people glaze over them. You can also use geographic targeting so your ads won't constantly appear in every country or region.

Promoted Trends

Another great way to get maximum exposure for your company is to use Promoted Trends. Twitter Trends is the real-time view of the most popular Twitter conversations. When you promote a trend, a hashtag of your choice appears at the top of the Twitter Trends list. When people click on the hashtag, they'll be redirected to the conversations using your hashtag. Figure 6–4 on page 90 shows you an example of a Promoted Trend.

Enhanced Profile Pages

An enhanced profile page is a new Twitter feature that increases your brand's Twitter presence. You can prominently feature important information about your company in

FIGURE 6–4. A Promoted Trend from American Express

the header of your Twitter page. You can even include a clickable link to your website which is not available on regular Twitter pages. The best feature of your enhanced profile page is it is completely public. This means users can view it without joining or logging into Twitter, and your enhanced profile page is indexed by Google and will appear in Google search results. Enhanced profile pages are currently available on a very limited basis but they will be rolled out in the coming months. Figure 6–5 on page 91 shows the new enhanced profile page for Coca-Cola.

Twitter API

In case you are not familiar with the term API, it stands for "application program interface." Don't be intimidated by this technical jargon. In layman's terms, an API is a piece of code that acts like a customized key to Twitter's database. You get the code from Twitter and easily add it into your website. This lets you display your live Twitter feed on your website, add Twitter buttons so people can easily follow you, and buttons so people can easily ReTweet your content. If you are familiar with APIs or know someone who is, you can obtain a Twitter API key and pull Twitter data directly from the Twitter database into your custom applications. This lets you analyze your Twitter activity and your competitors' activity.

Most small-business owners don't have the expertise or the need to use the Twitter API to analyze their Twitter activity. The Twitter tools we review in Chapter 8 will provide all of the data you need.

FIGURE 6–5. The Enhanced Profile Page for Coca-Cola

I do recommend visiting the Twitter for Websites page at https://dev.twitter.com/docs/twitter-for-websites, where you can create and download custom Twitter buttons for your website. Figure 6–6 on page 92 shows you the available Twitter buttons you can add to your website to increase engagement with your website visitors. These buttons make it easy for others to follow you and to share your content with their social network. You can also embed your Tweets into your website which also increases engagement with your web visitors.

CONCLUSION

Creating and executing your Twitter strategy is essential to your Twitter success. Your Twitter strategy should be constantly evolving as Twitter grows and adds more functionality. Review and update your Twitter strategy on a quarterly basis to make sure you're getting the most from your efforts.

In the next chapter I'm going to teach you some advanced Twitter techniques. This is where you will learn how to become a Twitter Power User and accelerate the reach of your marketing efforts.

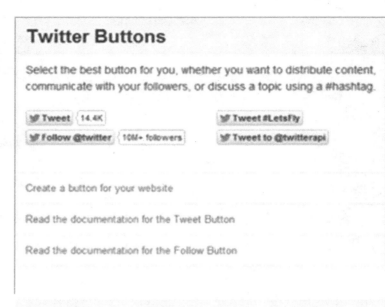

Embedded Tweets

Tweets are dynamic and interactive media with authors, mentions, @people, #topics, pictures & videos. Now you can embed them on your website with just one line of code.

Learn how to embed a Tweet

FIGURE 6–6. Twitter for Websites Lets You Easily Add Twitter to Your Website

Advanced Twitter

By now you should have a complete Twitter profile, followed some people, and have some people following you back. A few of you may have even started Tweeting. How does it feel to be part of the Twitterverse? Pretty good, I bet.

Now it's time to take off the training wheels and move into advanced Twitter. Keep practicing the basics, like Tweeting regularly and looking for good people to follow, while I introduce you to some advanced Twitter tools and techniques.

TWITTER LISTS

A Twitter List is Twitter's version of a group you might find on Facebook or LinkedIn except you don't have to ask or be invited to join. You can create a topic-specific list of people you follow so you can easily see their Tweets, outside of your Tweet stream. You can also follow others' lists.

Lists offer you a way to group together other users on Twitter so that you can see what they're up to. Lists aren't just static listings of users. They are curated Twitter streams of the latest Tweets from the list members.

You can create a list that groups people together, like team members. You can get a quick overview of the group's conversations by viewing that list's page. The list's page includes a complete Tweet stream for everyone on the list. Lists allow you to organize the people you're following into groups, and you can also include people you're not following.

Creating Twitter Lists

It's easy to create your own Twitter list. In your Twitter Settings, go to Lists as seen in Figure 7–1.

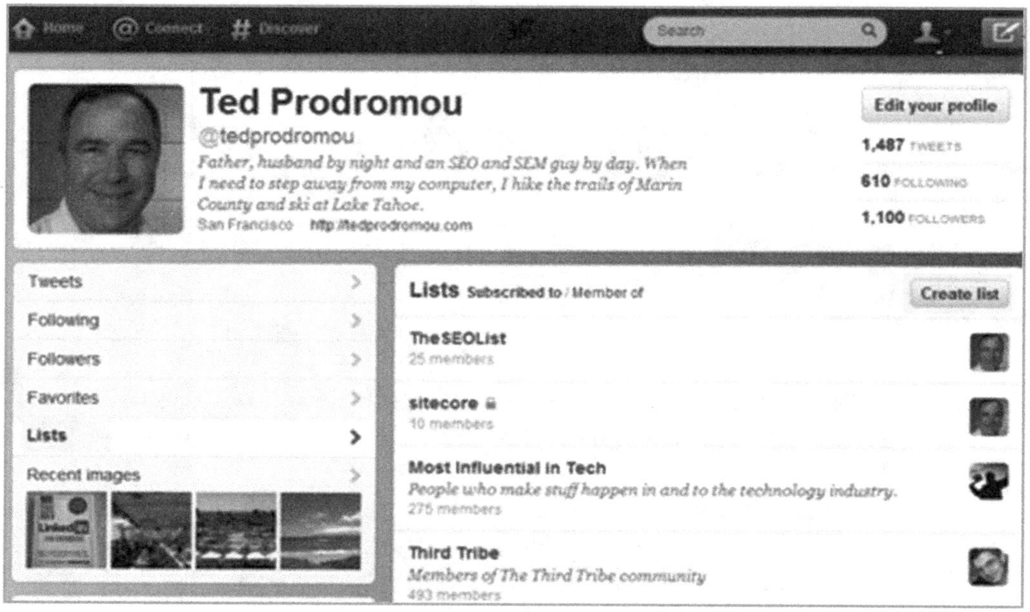

FIGURE 7–1. You Can Create and Manage Twitter Lists in Your Twitter Settings

Click on Create List and you will be prompted to enter a list name and description as you see in Figure 7–2 on page 95. You can also make your new Twitter list Public or Private. When you create a Public list, other Twitter members can subscribe to your list and view the conversations by those on your list but they can't modify your list. If you create a private list, only people you approve can subscribe to the list and view the activity.

The next step is to add people to your new list. To add people to your list, click on the Following link on your Twitter home page then click on the headshot icon shown in Figure 7–3 on page 95.

Select Add or Remove From Lists . . . and select the list you want to add them to or Create a List as shown in Figure 7–4 on page 96. As you see people in your Twitterstream that you want to add to your list, repeat this process.

FIGURE 7-2. Creating Your New Twitter List

FIGURE 7-3. Adding People to Your Twitter List

How to Subscribe To/Follow Other People's Lists

You can easily subscribe to other people's lists.

- Click on the Lists tab when viewing someone's profile.
- Select which list you'd like to subscribe to.
- From the list page, click Subscribe to follow the list. You can follow lists without following the individual users in that list.

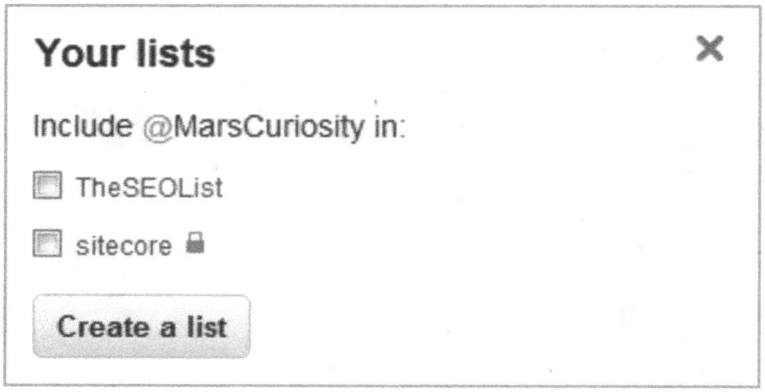

FIGURE 7–4. Selecting the Appropriate List When Adding People to Your Twitter List

Let's say you are a search engine optimization consultant and you use Twitter to discuss SEO, as I do. I created a list called TheSEOList, which appears as http://twitter.com/tedprodromou/theseolist. I add SEO experts to the Twitter list so I can easily see the hot SEO topics of the day. When I want to view just the Tweets from the members of my list I visit my list at http://twitter.com/tedprodromou/theseolist. The Tweets from the members of my list won't get lost in my Tweet stream, which makes it easier to keep up with the hot topics. I don't even have to be following the members of my list so my Twitterstream remains clean but I can view hot topics using my Twitter lists. Figure 7–5 on page 97 shows my Twitter list called TheSEOList.

Why Use Twitter Lists?

There are many reasons for creating lists. The more people you follow, the more Tweets you see in your Tweet stream, so it's harder to follow certain conversations. Lists help you filter out some of the noise when you're working closely with a group of people.

Create a Group

Twitter lists help your organize the Tweet streams of people you follow. You can create lists based on certain topics so you can keep up with the latest conversations about that topic. If you were a social media consultant, you could create lists of social media experts. One list could be for Facebook experts, another list for LinkedIn experts, and another, for Twitter experts.

By viewing these lists, you easily see what all of these social media experts are Tweeting about.

FIGURE 7–5. My Twitter List TheSEOList Lets Me Organize Twitter Discussions about SEO

Recommend Industry Experts

You can create a public list of people you think other Twitter users should follow in specific industries. People can follow your list and see what these industry experts are Tweeting about. This gives you credibility because you created the list of experts for others to use and they can see what the experts are talking about without having to actually follow these experts. When you don't follow someone, you won't see their Tweets in your Tweet stream, but you can keep track of them by viewing the list occasionally.

Follow People You Aren't Following

When you follow a Twitter List, you're not actually following every user on the list, but following the entire list—those users' Tweets aren't added to your main stream. You can then visit that list and view its Tweet stream. That's why you can also use Lists to follow people without really following them. For example, if there are users whose Tweets you'd like to follow, but whom you don't necessarily want in your main Twitter stream (perhaps they Tweet too often for your liking), you can add them to a list and then check up on their latest Tweets every once in a while by viewing your list.

If you are looking for Twitter lists about a specific topic or interest, visit www.listorius.com. Figure 7–6 shows you some of the categories of lists you can follow. You can also add your own lists to Listorious so others can follow your list.

Listorious

Search over 2 million top Twitter users		Search

activism	charity	entertainment	media	progressive	technology
art	children	environment	music	science	travel
business	climate	food	news	socialmedia	twitter
celebrities	education	health	politics	sports	writers

Tags   Add Yourself   Add a Twitter List   Inbox   Sign in with Twitter   About

FIGURE 7–6. Some of the Twitter List Categories Available on Listorius

CREATING VIRAL TWEETS

Everyone has forwarded a funny email or a link to a hilarious YouTube video to their friends. We also forward information we think is important or relevant to our friends. When content is forwarded numerous times, it's considered viral content. So what makes content viral, and better yet, how do we create viral content? Wouldn't you love to be able to create content that's forwarded over and over again?

Creating viral content isn't as hard as you think. Getting a million views on your YouTube video may be a little tricky, but getting your customers to forward or ReTweet your content isn't that hard. Here are some ideas to help you create viral content.

Add a Call to Action

Remember when I talked about creating a strategy for every Tweet and promotion you do? Every Tweet should be done for a specific reason and should include a call to action. Every time you Tweet, you want your followers to ReTweet it so it spreads throughout the Twitterverse. This enables your message to reach more people than just your followers. When someone ReTweets your Tweet, it's seen by your followers and the followers of the person who ReTweeted it. Every time your message is ReTweeted, it expands into another network of Twitter users, accelerating faster and faster each time.

You know the old saying, "Ask and you shall receive." Ask people to ReTweet your Tweet and they will most of the time. When you have a message you really want people to ReTweet just add, "Please RT" or "Please ReTweet" to your Tweet. This works amazingly well if you don't overuse it. Take a look at Figure 7–7 on page 100 and look at how well RT works versus ReTweet in your message.

Some other words you can use in your Tweet that will encourage ReTweeting are:

- Check this out . . .
- You should really follow . . .
- Please vote
- "What do you think of . . ." or "Where is the best place to . . ."
- I need some help . . .

Timing

You need to experiment to see when you will get the best response from your followers. From my experience, a business-related Tweet receives the most traction on weekdays during working hours, which makes perfect sense. If you are Tweeting something

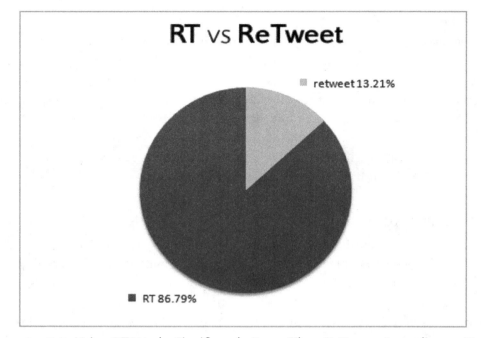

FIGURE 7–7. Using RT Works Significantly Better Than ReTweet, According to Dan Zarrella. *Source*: www.danzarrella.com

not business-related, you can get a good response just about any time. Again, this depends on your followers, where they are located, and their interests. When you do get a ReTweet, track it in a spreadsheet and note the day, time, and the content of your Tweet. This will let you see patterns and determine the best time to Tweet to your followers.

You can also use SocialBro to determine the best time to Tweet. In the Tools section of SocialBro, choose Best Time to Tweet and the program will assess your followers' behavior and tell you what time they are likely to be online and Tweeting.

Links

According to Dan Zarrella of HubSpot, his research shows that Tweets with links in them are ReTweeted almost 70 percent of the time. Figure 7–8 on page 101 shows you Dan's research results.

Social Proof

When you see a great movie, what do you do? I bet you tell your friends about it. Then your friends go see it and tell their friends about it. Word spreads faster and faster

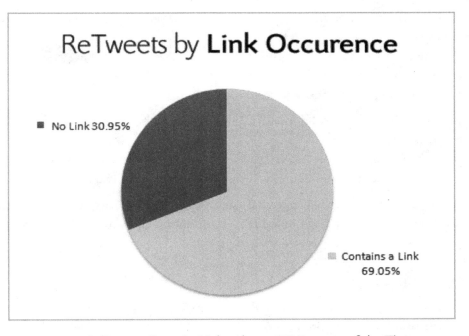

FIGURE 7–8. ReTweets Contain Links Almost 70 Percent of the Time. *Source:* www.danzarrella.com

as each friend tells their network of friends. The momentum turns into frenzy and suddenly the movie turns into a blockbuster.

This is called social proof, also known as social influence. We tend to think if something is okay for one person, then it's okay for us because we assume they have more knowledge about the subject.

Because of the social proof phenomenon, the likelihood of a Tweet being ReTweeted increases dramatically each time it is ReTweeted. The momentum builds with each ReTweet and suddenly you have a blockbuster Tweet!

Add Value

You build your reputation on social media by providing value to your network. The adage "The more you give the more you receive" holds true in social media. Follow some big names in Twitter like @CarrieWilkerson, @ChrisBrogan and @BrianSolis and see how they add value to their networks. They give way more than they receive. You never see them dominating a conversation on Twitter or speaking negatively about a person. They are constantly providing great resources and product reviews to their followers. Notice how many ReTweets they receive after they Tweet a good resource or their opinion on a topic. Their Tweets are always ReTweeted hundreds of times by others.

Take note of what the successful Twitter users Tweet about that gets ReTweeted. Follow their lead and use the same Twitter style as they do. Here are some ideas about what you can Tweet about that will receive a lot of ReTweets:

- How-to information and instructional content
- Breaking news
- Tech warnings such as viruses, Facebook scams, or product updates
- Contests and discount coupons for products or services you enjoy

As you see, it's not hard to create viral Tweets when you think from the perspective of giving instead of receiving. Provide valuable information and support to your followers and your Tweets will be ReTweeted with regularity.

LEAD GENERATION

Twitter is a great tool for finding potential customers, whether your company sells business-to-business (B2B) or business-to-consumer (B2C). The easiest way to generate leads on the internet is to create an interesting free report or informational video that talks about one of your customers' biggest problems. In the report or video, you focus on the "why" they need to change something in their business to become more successful or profitable. The report or video doesn't have to solve their problem. You just want to focus on telling them why they need to change the way they are doing business if they want to see better results.

You'll need a few things to set up your lead-generation system. I'm assuming if you are going to do a video that you have a high-definition camera and know how to use it. Here's what else you need to generate leads online.

- A URL shortener that tracks the number of clicks
- A landing page on your website
- An email autoresponder program so you can create a web form to capture leads

The process is very simple and can be broken down into 14 steps.

1. If you don't know what your customer's biggest problem is (shame on you if you don't know!) survey your customers and ask them. You can also Tweet the question to your followers and see how they respond.
2. If you don't have one already, create a product or service that solves their biggest problem.
3. Create a free report or informational video that focuses on the "why" they have that problem and why they need to change something in their business to overcome the problem. You'll tell them how to solve the problem after they hire you.

4. Create a landing page on your website or blog. In Figure 6–1 on page 80, I showed you a landing page, which is a page on your website that doesn't have a navigational menu or anything that would distract the web visitor from reading the content on the page. The objective of a landing page is to get the visitor to fill out the web form so they'll receive their content from you. You don't want them to get distracted by clicking on links to other pages of your website

5. The only content on the landing page is a headline describing their biggest problem and a few paragraphs describing what they will learn about their problem by reading the report or by viewing the video. The purpose of the landing page content is to get them to fill out the web form. You don't want to talk about your product or service that will solve their problem until later. Right now, you just want to collect their contact information.

6. You need an email autoresponder program such as www.aweber.com or www.infusionsoft.com so you can set up web forms to collect names and email addresses. You don't need to collect more than that.

7. Set up your email campaign in your email autoresponder program and create the web form. Install the web form on your landing page so you can collect their first name and email address. Your email autoresponder program will have detailed instructions to help you set up your email campaign and web form.

8. Create a "thank you" page on your website or blog that uses the same template as your landing page. This is the page they will be redirected to after they fill out their web form. They can download their free report or watch the video on this page.

9. Now you want to send a Tweet with a link to the landing page. The Tweet should mention the problem they are having and hint that there is a solution to their problem. You want to use a URL shortener that tracks the clicks on the link. Hoot-Suite, www.bitly.com, and www.budurl.com all shorten and track your links.

10. After they fill out the web form, you will have their contact information. In your email autoresponder program, you can set up a series of automatic email messages. You will create one message that will be sent immediately after they fill out the web form thanking them for joining your email list. You should also tell them how to download their report or where to watch the video.

11. Set up a series of five or six emails that will be sent every other day. The first couple of emails will talk about why they have the problem and that many businesses have the same problem. You can share some stories about other businesses that struggled with the same problem and overcame it with your help.

12. The emails should transition into "what" they can do to solve the problem. Don't tell them "how" to solve the problem yet. You can create more free reports

or videos that teach them how they can solve the problem by making changes to their business. Don't try to sell them your product or service yet. Just get them focused on what they can change in their business.

13. The last few emails should start talking about "how" they can solve their problem. Once they start understanding how the problem can be solved, you can start offering your products and services that will solve their problem quickly.

14. Repeat the process over and over for each problem your customers have so you can build an email database of customers and prospects for your business. This way you can build a relationship with them and retain them as customers for a long time.

That's lead generation in a nutshell. Determine their problem, tell them why they need to change something to solve the problem, tell them what they need to do to solve the problem, and then tell them how to solve the problem using your products or services.

BUILDING YOUR BRAND OR BUSINESS

Twitter is a great tool to build your brand and spread the word about your business. Twitter's reach is extensive, and word travels fast. Here are some tips for building your brand on Twitter.

- *Use your brand name as your Twitter name.* This seems obvious, but I see many companies not using their brand name as their Twitter name. They use a cute Twitter name that isn't related to their brand name.
- *Use your logo as your Twitter picture.* Again, very obvious, but some companies don't use their logo for some reason.
- *Send Tweets that provide useful information to customers and prospects.* Always add a link to more information on your website. It should be a page on your website that adds value to the Tweet but doesn't require them to fill out a web form to view the information. This complements your lead-generation Tweets. You don't want to make people fill out a web form every time or they may get frustrated.
- *Send Tweets to new blog posts or videos.* You can also send Tweets to older blog posts and videos that are still relevant.
- *You should Tweet 10 to 20 times a day to keep your brand name in the Twitter stream.* You can schedule the Tweets that have links to valuable content and complement that with 5 to 10 personalized Tweets where you are interacting with other Twitter users.

■ *Create a persona for your Twitter presence so people will get to know your brand.* Investopedia defines brand personality as, "A set of human characteristics that are attributed to a brand name. A brand personality is something to which the consumer can relate, and an effective brand will increase its brand equity by having a consistent set of traits. This is the added value that a brand gains, aside from its functional benefits." There are five main types of brand personalities: excitement, sincerity, ruggedness, competence, and sophistication.

- *Excitement.* It's easy to spot a person who's excited on Twitter. These people love life and they love everything they do. They also love to share their excitement with the Twitterverse and it's fun to follow these people. Their Tweets will almost always uplift you.
- *Sincerity.* We all know the sincere people in our lives. They really care about you and your well-being. They Tweet the same way by always being genuine, caring, and sincere when they converse with others on Twitter.
- *Ruggedness.* These are the tough guys who never shed a tear. Their Tweets sound like John Wayne or Clint Eastwood confronting their adversaries and never backing down. You'll never see a hint of compassion or sympathy from rugged Tweeters.
- *Competence.* This is a well-educated, knowledgeable person who loves to Tweet information that will impress others. They love to share their knowledge and use big words in their Tweets, which can be challenging with the 140-character limit.
- *Sophistication.* Paris Hilton and Kim Kardashian are sophisticated Tweeters. They love to Tweet pictures of their shopping trips and expensive cars, and let you know they're eating in the finest restaurants.

From my experience, consistency is the key to success when building your brand on Twitter. People get used to seeing your brand and persona on Twitter and look forward to your Tweets once they get to know you. You need to be engaging and entertaining when you Tweet to capture their attention. People become raving fans when you consistently provide valuable information and entertain them.

"ADVERTISING" ON TWITTER: PROMOTED PRODUCTS

For years, Twitter has been trying to figure out how to generate revenue so it can continue to grow and eventually go public. The obvious choice is to offer advertising, but nothing kills a popular website like too many ads. Twitter has been experimenting with a variety of advertising and revenue models, and it looks like their series of Promoted products may be the answer.

Three tools make up the Twitter Promote Products suite. They are Promoted Accounts, Promoted Tweets, and Promoted Trends. Let's explore the three products so you can see how they could help promote your business or your brand.

These products are fairly new and very expensive to get started, so they are primarily being used by large businesses now. An entry-level campaign will cost at least $15,000 for a three-month campaign. Eventually Twitter will offer more affordable advertising options so small businesses can take advantage of Twitter's popularity and volume of web traffic.

Promoted Accounts

The purpose of Promoted Accounts is to help you to add more influencers and advocates to your brand. You can use Promoted Accounts to build brand loyalty, increase exposure for your campaigns, and to grow your earned media. Earned media, owned media, and paid media are terms used to help you measure the success of your social media campaigns. Earned media often refers specifically to publicity gained through editorial influence, whereas social media refers to publicity gained through grassroots action on the internet. Owned media is a media channel that you own, like your website or your blog. Paid media is when a brand pays money to leverage a media channel like online advertising.

When you run a Promoted Accounts campaign on Twitter, your Twitter account will appear as a Promoted entry at the top of the Who to Follow box on targeted people's Twitter page. In Figure 7–9 on page 107 you see a sample Promoted Accounts campaign.

Promoted Accounts campaigns are targeted by interests. Twitter algorithmically determines the interests of the people you follow. The advertisers refine the algorithmic targeting with interest-based keywords, resulting in an average retention rate of 90 percent, which is incredible. You can also choose to do geo-targeting by country and/or by metro areas in the United States. You are charged on a cost–per-follow (CPF) basis. This means you only pay when someone becomes a follower from clicking on your ad. The average price per follower is between two and three U.S. dollars, depending on the competiveness of the market you are targeting.

Promoted Tweets

Promoted Tweets is another Twitter advertising option where you create Tweets that are displayed to your target market. The benefits of Promoted Tweets include amplified conversations, driving engagement, and leveraging real-time intent.

An *amplified conversation* is just what it sounds like. By promoting a Twitter conversation with a Promoted Tweet, you are expanding the range of the conversation exponentially.

FIGURE 7–9. A Sample Promoted Accounts Campaign for Jaguar USA

Driving engagement is similar to amplifying the conversation. You are engaging significantly more people by using Promoted Tweets to spread your message. If you simply Tweet a message about your brand, your followers will see your Tweet and it will appear on the Twitter timeline where a few others may see it. When you promote your Tweet, you will engage a lot more people because your message will appear in Twitter streams that contain similar keywords that are in your Tweet. It's like renting a billboard at a very busy intersection where everyone who passes through will see your message.

Leveraging real-time intent through Promoted Tweets lets you get your message out to others at specific times. For example, if your company is a major sponsor at a tradeshow, you can leverage that sponsorship by using Promoted Tweets during the event. Your Promoted Tweets will appear in real time and will be promoting your message to everyone who is following the tradeshow's hashtag.

Your Promoted Tweets will drive targeted traffic to promotions on your website or your blog. Promoted Tweets are displayed in Timelines and in Search results and are designated as Promoted by your Twitter username. Figure 7–10 on page 108 shows a Mother's Day promotion by @WittleBee.

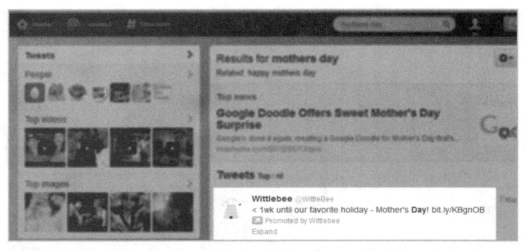

FIGURE 7–10. A Promoted Tweet by @WittleBee for a Mother's Day Promotion

You can target specific countries and metropolitan areas for regional and local messages, or run your campaign worldwide.

Promoted Tweets are charged on a cost-per-engagement (CPE) pricing model where you are only charged when a user engages by taking action on your Tweet. If they click on your link, Favorite your Tweet, ReTweet, or Reply to your Tweet, you will be charged anywhere from 50 cents to $1.50 per engagement. The engagement rate is approximately 1 to 3 percent, which is very similar to other online advertising campaigns. Twitter uses a built-in ad quality filter that combines relevance, engagement, and the age of a Tweet to make sure your ad is displayed to the appropriate audience.

Promoted Trends

Promoted Trends is another form of Twitter advertising. Twitter Trends is one of the most popular sections of Twitter.com so your ad will receive a lot of attention. You can use Promoted Trends to:

- Make a company announcement
- Seed a conversation
- Kick off an online or offline event

As you see in Figure 7–11, page 109, a Promoted Trends campaign for #HappyMothersDay is well placed on the Twitter page.

Here are some facts about the Promoted Trends campaigns.

Fixed Placement

- Exclusive unit in the Trends module on the user's home timeline page

FIGURE 7–11. Promoted Trends Campaign for #HappyMothersDay

- 25,000,000 average daily U.S. impressions
- Average engagement rate is .3 percent on the Trend, 5 to 7 percent on the related Promoted Tweet

Increased Demand

- One advertiser per 24-hour day
- Fixed price for U.S. Promoted Trend is $120,000 reserved on a first-come, first-served basis for a given date

Promoted Trends campaigns are not cheap, but they are very effective for medium to large businesses. You receive exclusive placement for 24 hours and over 25 million impressions in the United States, which is tremendous exposure for your brand.

CONTESTS

Twitter contests are a great way you can use to find targeted followers who are interested in the content, products, and service. Twitter contests are easy to set up and run, but you should carefully plan them to make sure you attract the right people to your contest.

What Is a Twitter Contest?

A Twitter contest is essentially a marketing campaign that you use to get people to follow you and Tweet a predefined message. When they Tweet your message, they are automatically entered into a drawing to win a prize. The prizes are usually awarded to people who follow you and/or people who Tweeted your predefined message.

The results of Twitter contests are usually excellent if you plan them properly. The people who follow you during the contest usually stay engaged with you longer than other followers and they tend to take more action by Tweeting, ReTweeting, and Replying to your Tweets. They seem to get a sense that we are in this together and they go out of their way to support you and your company. They also tend to become frequent visitors of your website and other social media communities like your Facebook and LinkedIn pages.

The best thing about Twitter contests is that you can expect to see a 20 to 25 percent increase in your followers, and they will be very targeted followers. People will not participate in a Twitter contest if they aren't interested in your product or service.

How to Create a Successful Twitter Contest

Obviously the goal of most Twitter contests is to increase the number of targeted followers. Targeted followers are an extension of your marketing department and they help spread the word about your products and services for free. When a third party spreads positive comments about your products or services, it gives your company credibility and helps sell your products.

You also want to collect contestants' contact information during your Twitter campaign so you can nurture your new leads and eventually turn them into customers. You collect their contact information by enticing them to fill out a web form on your website or blog.

You want to attract targeted followers when you run a Twitter campaign. It won't help you if you attract thousands of new followers who are only interested in the prize you are giving away.

There are several ways to attract targeted followers during your Twitter campaign:

- Have a clear goal for your contest. What are you trying to achieve with your Twitter contest? Are you trying to generate new leads? Are you generating traffic for a new website or blog? Are you announcing a new product and you want to generate a buzz?

- You need to have a clear goal and outcome for your Twitter contest or you will be disappointed with your results. The clearer your goal is, the better your results will be.
- Choose prizes carefully. This is where people make some of their biggest mistakes when they conduct a Twitter contest. Your prize should match the goal for your contest. If you are trying to generate more targeted followers, offering a large cash prize isn't the right prize. Offering a $1,000 prize will attract a lot of new followers, but they may not be targeted. In fact many of your new followers will be participating in the contest just to win the $1,000, not to support your company.

If you are trying to attract landscape artists as followers, you could offer an autographed book of landscape pictures or artist accessories as your prize. This would be a more effective way to attract targeted followers than offering a large cash prize.

When you create a plan for your Twitter contest, it needs to do two things:

1. Encourage people in your niche to participate
2. Discourage people who aren't in your niche from participating

This may seem obvious to you but it's imperative that you design your contest properly and choose appropriate prizes so you attract the right people. Choosing the right prizes that appeal to your targeted Twitter audience will make your contest more successful.

Offer Prizes from Partners or Associates

A great way to generate even more buzz with your Twitter contest is to cooperate it with one of your partner companies or associates. You can expand your Twitter network even further by co-promoting a campaign so both companies benefit. Your company could be the primary in the Twitter contest and you could offer a prize donated by your partner company. This approach will grow your Twitter followers while providing publicity and exposure for your partner company, a win-win scenario for all.

When you reach out to partners or associates to ask them to participate in a Twitter contest, explain to them how they will benefit, how a Twitter contest works, and the role they will play. Let them know they will receive a lot of publicity, web traffic, and hopefully lots of new customers. When they donate one of the prizes for the contest, people will get to experience their product or service and will in turn tell their friends about their experience.

Feature Your Sponsors

You will benefit most from your contest if you focus on your sponsor more than you focus on your company. Make them the center of attention in your promotional campaigns and give them as much publicity as possible. Link to their blog and website as much as possible. Go out of your way in your contest promotions to thank them for donating the valuable prize. Rave about the value of the prize and how great it would be to win. When the sponsor sees how supportive you are, they will become more enthusiastic about the contest and promote it like crazy to their customers and prospects. The more they promote the contest, the more followers you get who in turn could become new customers for you. Provide your sponsor as much value as you can and your contest will be a huge success.

How Long Should the Contest Be?

People frequently ask me how long to run their Twitter campaigns. Of course my answer is, "It depends." I'm not trying to cop out and not answer the question. It depends on your objective for the campaign.

Some contests work best if you run them for a very limited time. For example, if you are running a Valentine's Day contest, it doesn't make sense to run it for two or three weeks. That's way too long. Valentine's Day is only on our radar for a few days, maybe a week. I'm sure some women think about it for a few weeks and most men only think of it for a day or so. The optimal time for a Valentine's Day contest is about a week. You want to give the contest time to build up and generate a big buzz but you don't want to drag it out too long. You want to create a sense of urgency so people will want to get in before it's too late.

You can run some contests for longer periods of time and still create that sense of urgency. Every year companies like Turbo Tax and H&R Block run contests for a month before taxes are due on April 15. They give away copies of their tax software every day. I remember a few years ago, Turbo Tax was giving away one copy of Turbo Tax at 7 P.M. every night. The number of Tweets using their hashtag spiked dramatically at that time every day. To win the software you just had to Tweet something about taxes and use their hashtag #TurboTax. The winner was chosen randomly from the thousands of Tweets that occurred at 7 P.M. They did this every day for a month and the contests were a huge success.

Another approach you may want to try is to run a contest for 10 days if your customers spend a lot of time online on weekends. You start the contest on a Friday and run it for two full weekends and the week in between. This gives you plenty of time to generate momentum for the contest. You could even give away smaller prizes on the first weekend and lead up to a grand prize that would be given out on the last day.

Play around with some small contests so you get a sense of how long you can hold your followers' interest. Some niche markets have a short attention span while others will pay attention for an extended period of time.

Track Your Campaigns

This is another obvious step in running a successful Twitter contest, but I'm always surprised by the number of people who don't track their results. Always track all of your marketing efforts and remember every marketing effort should be done for a reason.

It's important to use appropriate tools to measure your Twitter contest. If the objectives of your Twitter contest are to increase followers, increase ReTweets, and generate leads, you need a tool that can measure these statistics. You may have to use more than one tool to measure your results. In this example you could use a tool like HootSuite or HubSpot to measure the increase in the number of followers and ReTweets. To measure the leads generated by your contest, you could set up a new campaign in an email autoresponder program like Aweber or Constant Contact to capture your new leads. The key is to determine the appropriate measurement tool and test it before you launch your Twitter contest. I like to use multiple tools to measure my contests to make sure I'm accurately measuring the results. I use HootSuite as my primary measurement tool and I'll use a tool like SocialBro or TwitGraph for backup.

Celebrate the Winners

When your contest ends, it's important to reach out to the winners on Twitter and via email to let them know that they won as soon as possible. Once they respond, I let the Twitterverse know who won. It's important to wait until they respond to you to confirm that they are a real person and not a Twitterbot. It would be very embarrassing if the winner of your contest was a Twitterbot and you announced it to the world. That could have a negative effect on your credibility.

I usually give the winner a few days to respond before I choose another winner. If you wait too long to announce the winner, your contest will lose momentum and people may be reluctant to participate in future contests. Make it very clear in the contest rules that the winner must respond in a certain timeframe or another winner will be selected. This helps avoid any confusion and negative publicity if the original winner is slow to respond to you.

Once you confirm the winner, it's time to celebrate! Announce the winner publicly on Twitter, on the contest's web page, your blog, Facebook, LinkedIn, and your other social communities. You can even send out a press release announcing the winner of your contest. Make a big deal about announcing the winner. The more publicity you generate, the more popular your future contests will be.

When your contest is complete, take time to review its results. Did you meet your goals? What worked and what didn't? What could you do better in your next contest? It's important to review your contest in detail so you can make your next one even better.

It's also very important to follow up with your new leads in a timely manner. I also like to welcome my new followers with a personal message if possible.

Creating a Great ReTweet

The contest entry criteria for a Twitter contest is usually:

- Contestants must follow you on Twitter
- Contestants must ReTweet a specific message

You want to create a great message for them to ReTweet so you generate a buzz for your contest and promote your sponsor (if you have one).

An example of a good ReTweet message would be:

RT @YourTwitterID Win a $1500 autographed web marketing guide courtesy of @YourSponsorTwitterID http://bit.ly/LWN31T #hashtag

Your message should have the following elements:

- Your message should be less than 140 characters to give people room to add their personal comments to the ReTweet.
- Begin with something other than @YourTwitterID so the ReTweet will be treated like a Reply instead of a Mention. If you begin the ReTweet with @YourTwitterId it will only be seen by your followers.
- Use your Twitter ID in the message so people will follow you.
- Mention a brief summary of the prize.
- Mention your sponsor or their Twitter ID in the message and make it clear they are providing the prize.
- Add a trackable link that is shortened to the Tweet. You can use HootSuite or URL shorteners like Bitly or TinyURL.
- Add your contest hashtag to the ReTweet to help promote your contest.

The trick is to provide enough information about the contest, the prize, and your sponsor while leaving room for contestants to ReTweet the message. You will get the hang of it with a little practice. You can also test a few variations of the ReTweet message to see which performs best.

Launching Your Twitter Contest

It is essential that you plan the launch of your Twitter contest because you can't afford any hiccups once you start it. There are many potential points of failure so it's best to create a detailed launch plan with a complete checklist of tasks and responsibilities. It's also important to practice your launch by simulating the tasks as a team or by doing a small launch to make sure your task list is complete.

Involve Your Sponsors in the Planning and Testing Process

Your sponsors are an integral part of your Twitter contest, so get them involved from the beginning. Work together to create your task list and assign responsibilities.

- Give them plenty of time to work on their contest tasks and make sure the contest prize will be ready well in advance. Make sure you know exactly what the prize will be, how and when it will be delivered, and set an expiration date if the prize is a service or a nontangible item.
- Never change the prize once the contest begins.
- Never change the rules once the contest begins. If you run into problems, note the issue and correct the problem in your next contest. If the problem is so severe that it can cause negative repercussions to your business or your sponsor, discuss the issue with your sponsor and determine the best way to proceed, minimizing the impact on your businesses. You should never hold a contest that could have serious consequences for your business, but sometimes unforeseen events do arise. Respond quickly and decisively if a problem arises.
- Work together with your sponsor to create a marketing plan for the event and distribute the tasks and costs accordingly. Make sure both parties clearly understand their roles and responsibilities.
- Set up your promotional web pages well in advance and test all links thoroughly. Nothing kills a promotional campaign faster than a slow or nonfunctional web page.
- Promote the contest constantly using scheduled Tweets and social media posts. Also spend a few minutes throughout the day engaging with other Twitter users to let them know about the contest. Have as many people as possible from both your company and your sponsor's company Tweeting about the contest. Recruit some friends and customers to help with the promotion to spread the word as far as you can.
- Take full responsibility for promoting the contest in case your sponsor fails to do any promotion. You are the primary beneficiary of the contest, so assume you will be doing all of the promotion. If your sponsor does help with the promotion, it will be an unexpected benefit.
- Never charge someone to participate in the contest or require them to purchase anything to gain entry into the contest. This can be illegal in some states so always keep your contests free to everyone.
- Follow Twitter's contest rules at all times. Twitter contests have become very popular, so Twitter created some simple contest rules:

Discourage the creation of multiple accounts. If your contest encourages people to create multiple accounts to better their chances of winning, you are in violation of Twitter's Terms of Service.

Discourage posting the same Tweet repeatedly. While it's OK to have one Tweet that everyone needs to use, you cannot encourage users to Tweet it multiple times to increase their chances of winning.

- Make sure you let the contest participants know to include an @reply to you so you will receive their entry.

Twitter contests are very effective when you set clear contest objectives, plan your contest carefully, measure your success, and test, test, and test again before you launch. Remember to make your contest fun and easy to enter so more people will participate.

CONCLUSION

You now know more about Twitter than the majority of Twitter users. The tricks you just learned will help you get the word out about your business so you can build a strong following and build long-lasting relationships. In the next chapter, I'm going to introduce you to some of my favorite Twitter tools that will help you use Twitter more efficiently and effectively. These tools will make Twitter easier to use and help you do more in less time.

Twitter Tools

Using Twitter is very easy, and accessing the application from www. twitter.com allows you to get started immediately after creating your account. However, Twitter use has grown exponentially since it's been integrated into other applications. These third-party applications enhance Twitter's capabilities and make it very easy for you to manage your Twitter experience from your desktop computer, your tablet computer, and your smartphone. We all carry our cell phones with us everywhere we go, so being able to Tweet and share our experiences while on the go has increased Twitter use substantially.

Let's explore some of the more popular Twitter applications now. There are new applications being developed every day, which is really exciting because it helps us stay connected with our followers and those people we are following.

TWEETDECK

TweetDeck is a cross-platform Twitter management tool developed on Adobe AIR. It has a user-friendly interface and runs on every system (Web, Mac, Linux, Windows, iOS, and Android).

TweetDeck enhances the Twitter experience by adding more flexibility, allowing advanced users to gain valuable insight into what's happening on

Twitter. TweetDeck started out as a web-based application but now gives you several options that allow you to access TweetDeck while on the go.

- *Web access.* You create your TweetDeck account at http://web.Tweetdeck.com where you can log in and use the browser-based version. Right now the browser-based version is limited to the Chrome and Safari browsers. If you only use Internet Explorer or Firefox, you can download the desktop application to run on your local computer.
- *Chrome app.* If you prefer to use the Chrome browser, you can go to the Chrome Web Store and install the TweetDeck app. The Chrome app works exactly like the web version but runs within the Chrome browser.
- *Desktop app.* If you prefer to use a desktop-based application, you can download the TweetDeck app for either the PC or Mac platform. You can download the Windows version directly from the TweetDeck site and the Mac version can be downloaded from the Apple App Store.

Your TweetDeck Account

Your TweetDeck account allows you to manage multiple social media accounts from one place. Once you set up your TweetDeck dashboard, your configuration is automatically synchronized when you log in from different computers. This allows you to manage all of your social media accounts from your desktop computer, your laptop, your tablet device, or your smartphone. When you log into your TweetDeck account, you are automatically signed into all of your social media accounts.

To sign up for a TweetDeck account:

Using your Chrome or Safari browser, go to http://web.Tweetdeck.com and click on Create Account, as shown in Figure 8–1 on page 119. If you use Internet Explorer or Firefox, you must download the desktop application first, and you will be prompted to create your account during the software installation process.

Enter your email address and password and your TweetDeck account is ready. Note: You must create a new account with TweetDeck even if you already have a Twitter account. Twitter recently purchased TweetDeck so they may integrate the accounts, but for now you need separate accounts.

TweetDeck automatically signs you into your account after you register. Now you can add multiple Twitter and Facebook accounts to your TweetDeck account. As you see in Figure 8–2 on page 120, you simply click on Add Twitter Account or Add Facebook Account.

FIGURE 8–1. The TweetDeck Login/Signup Screen

Let's add your Twitter account first. As soon as you click Add Twitter Account, TweetDeck will ask permission to authorize TweetDeck to use your Twitter account as shown in Figure 8–3, page 121. You learned about Twitter apps and permissions in Chapter 3 so I won't get into the details again. You can trust TweetDeck, so click on Authorize App. By authorizing the TweetDeck app, you are allowing TweetDeck to pull your Tweets from your timeline, see who you are following, update your Twitter profile, send Tweets for you, and access your direct messages. This lets you perform all of your Twitter actions from the TweetDeck application.

Once you click on Authorize app, your Twitter account will be integrated with TweetDeck and you can begin configuring your new dashboard. Your initial TweetDeck dashboard will launch and you will see three columns, Timeline, Interactions, and Messages.

Your Timeline is the same data you see in the middle column of your Twitter homepage. Also called your Twitter feed, it contains all of your Tweets and the Tweets

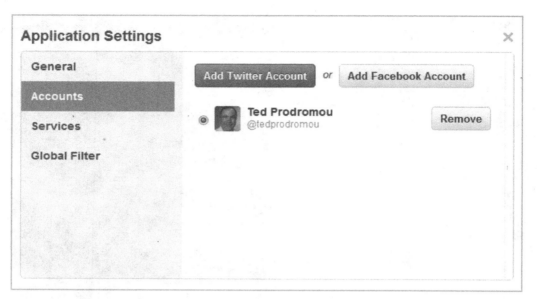

FIGURE 8–2. Adding Your Twitter and Facebook Accounts to TweetDeck

of the people you follow. It scrolls continuously with the latest data from your personal Twitterverse.

The Interactions column lets you know when others started following you and when you start following others. I use this column to determine if I want to follow someone back after they follow me. The first thing I do is review their profile to see if there is anything that grabs my attention. If they look interesting, I'll look at their Twitter stream. If they're Tweeting anything interesting, I will follow them. If they just ReTweet other people's Tweets, or just Tweet a bunch of links from an automated RSS feed, then I don't follow them. You can learn more about following people in Chapter 5.

Adding Columns

Instead of a single timeline like you see on www.twitter.com, TweetDeck lets you create columns to separate the content that interests you most from your Twitter feed. You can create a column that shows all your Mentions, the results of a search query, a list of Favorites, the latest Tweets from a hashtag, Twitter Trends, or the Tweets from someone you are following.

To Add a Column

Adding columns is simple. Click Add Column in the top navigation bar, which will open a menu that lets you choose from several column types. Figure 8–4 on page 122 shows you the column types you can choose.

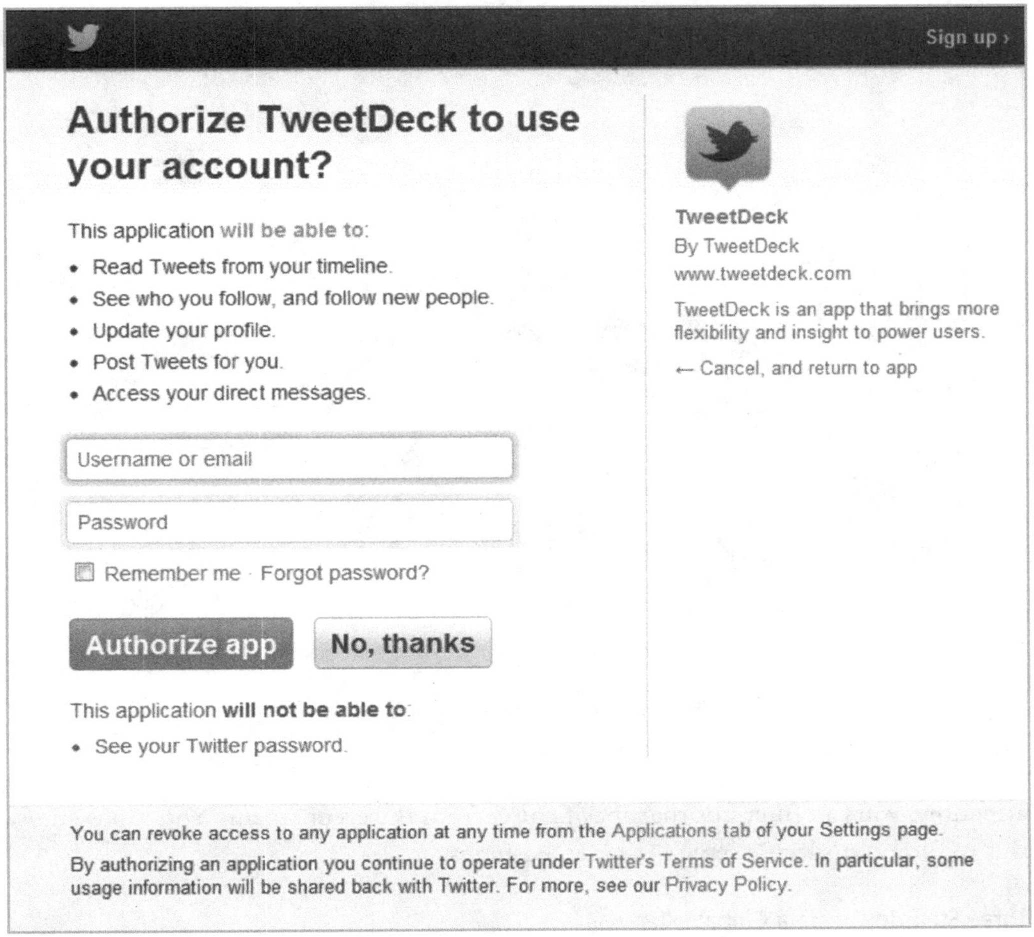

FIGURE 8–3. Authorizng TweetDeck to Access Your Twitter Account

After you've created your new column, you can click Back to add another column or click the [x] in the top right corner to close the menu. As you see, you can separate your Twitter feed data into columns of data, making it easier to keep in touch with trending topics or your favorite Tweeters.

Filtering Your Twitter Data

Very often, you may be overwhelmed with Twitter updates when you are following current event hashtags or hot topics. If you find you have too many unwanted updates filling up your columns, you can use the global filter to remove any content you're just not that interested in. If one person is Tweeting too many updates about an event they're

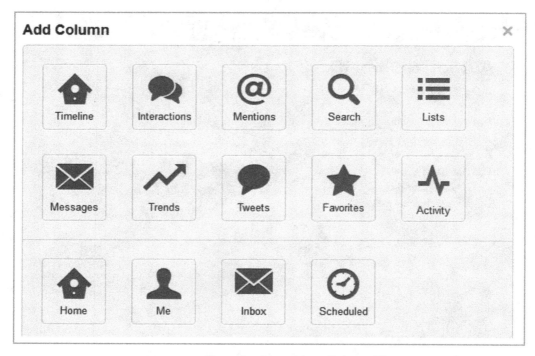

FIGURE 8–4. Choosing Your New Column Type

attending, you can filter out that specific user from the event stream. You can even use this to filter out specific services or even hashtags.

Three Steps to Create a Global Filter

1. Click the settings icon (looks like a gear cog) in the far right corner of the top navigation bar and select Settings.
2. Select Global Filter.
3. Choose your filter settings and select Add filter to finish.

Scheduling Tweets and Direct Messages

Scheduling Tweets is a great way to share relevant information with your followers. You can schedule Tweets to promote blog posts or information about an upcoming event at which you'll be speaking. I recommend scheduling a few Tweets per day to complement your live Tweeting, but don't overdo it.

To Schedule a New Tweet

Scheduling Tweets is very easy.

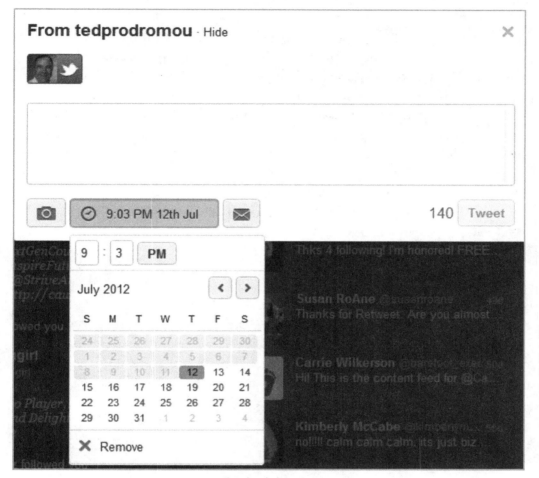

FIGURE 8–5. Scheduling Your Tweets

1. Click the *compose Tweet* icon (looks like a feather quill) in the top navigation bar.
2. Type in your desired message and click the time settings icon at the bottom of the pop-up composer to select a date and time (pictured in Figure 8–5).
3. When you're ready to send, click Tweet.

Once you've scheduled a date and time for your message, a new column will appear showing your Scheduled Tweets. This column will let you edit or delete your Tweets before they're sent. If you want to attach a photo to your Tweet, click the camera icon. To send a Direct Message, click the message icon, which looks like an envelope. Sometimes I'll schedule a Direct Message to a friend to remind them of an upcoming lunch or meeting.

Account Management

My favorite feature of TweetDeck is the ability to manage multiple Twitter accounts and my Facebook account from one dashboard. I add my personal Twitter account plus a few Twitter accounts from our company so I can monitor everything from one screen. It helps me see what's happening in the Twitterverse and respond quickly to Tweets posted by friends or dissatisfied customers. I also add my Facebook account so I can update my Facebook status without having to log into Facebook in another browser window.

Price: Free

Platforms: Desktop app for PC and Mac, web access via Chrome and Safari browser, apps for iPhone, iPad, and Android devices

HOOTSUITE

At first glance, HootSuite looks a lot like TweetDeck. Once you look under the hood, you see HootSuite is so much more than TweetDeck. Don't get me wrong. TweetDeck is a great tool and I've used it for years. It's perfect for an individual social media user who is active on both Twitter and Facebook. If you want to manage multiple social media accounts, like Twitter, Facebook, LinkedIn, and even your WordPress blog from one dashboard, then you need to look into HootSuite. Figure 8–6 on page 125 shows you the social media accounts you can manage from your HootSuite dashboard.

HootSuite does everything TweetDeck can do and much more. Here are a few additional features HootSuite brings to the table.

- HootSuite works with any web browser.
- You can also download apps for your tablet device and smartphone so you can take HootSuite everywhere you go.
- HootSuite does not have a downloadable app for your PC or Mac. Everything runs through the web browser or app so you see the same dashboard on every device.
- Dashboard tabs let you monitor your competitors on separate tabs. This lets you create custom columns for each competitor so you can monitor all of their social media accounts on one screen. You can also create custom tabs for industry thought leaders, target keywords, and industry news.
- HootSuite's Pro and Enterprise plans let you have multiple contributors to your social profiles without sharing passwords. You can assign messages to specific team members for follow-up and track responses. Every team member will use the same dashboard layout so everyone is monitoring the same Twitter feeds. They

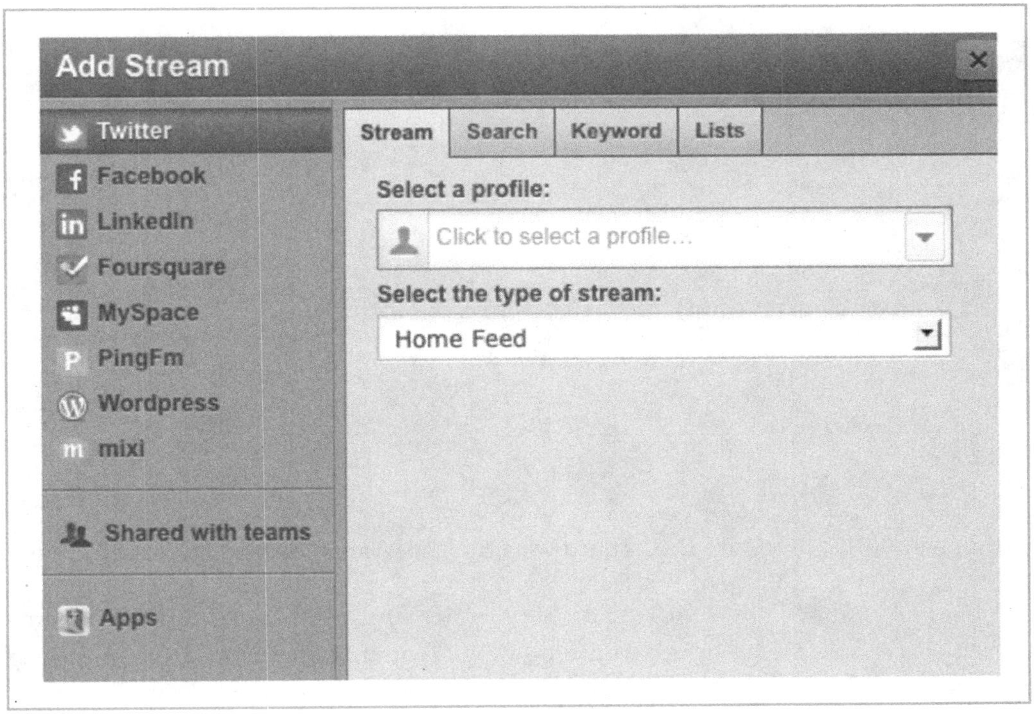

FIGURE 8–6. HootSuite Lets You Manage Numerous Social Media Accounts from One Dashboard

can also add custom columns to their own dashboard to monitor specific feeds related to their department or job function.

- Custom analytics are available.
- Create custom reports from over 30 individual report modules.
- Track brand sentiment and follower growth.
- Incorporate Facebook Insights and Google analytics.
- OW.ly URL shortener is built in so you can track click-through on links to get individual link and summary stats to measure the success of your messaging.
- Auto-update your profiles from your blog or news feed with RSS integration right into your HootSuite dashboard.
- There are multiple themes so you can change the colors and look of your Hoot-Suite dashboard.
- You can use Firefox and Chrome browser extensions so you can integrate Hoot-Suite into your browser and quickly Tweet links to web pages you are visiting.
- Multilanguage dashboard options include English, Japanese, Italian, and French, with more languages coming soon.

FIGURE 8–7. My HootSuite Dashboard with Multiple Tabs Organizing Twitter Feeds

Figure 8–7 shows my HootSuite dashboard. Across the top I have tabs for Featured Tweets, Facebook, LinkedIn, tedprodromou (my Twitter feed), competitors, following (people I follow), Miscellaneous, and Sitecore (the company I work for). From one screen I can manage multiple social media accounts, monitor multiple companies and Twitter users, and see the Featured Tweets.

Signing Up for HootSuite

The registration process for HootSuite is very simple. Go to www.HootSuite.com and fill out your email address, your full name, and password. Figure 8–8 shows you the HootSuite homepage where you can register for your free account.

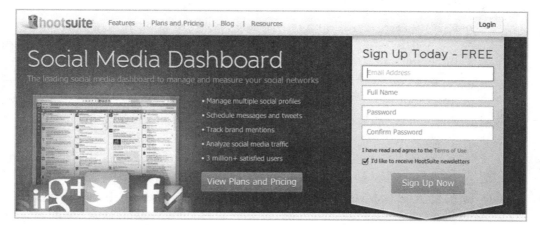

FIGURE 8–8. The HootSuite Homepage and Signup Form

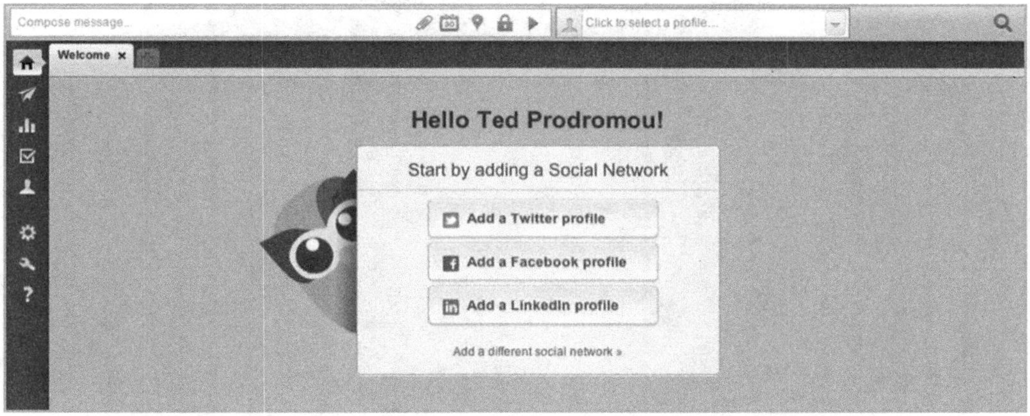

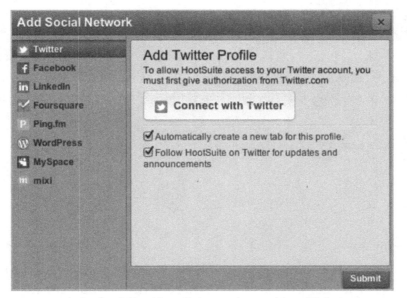

FIGURE 8–9. Adding Your Social Networks to HootSuite

Next, you add your social networks using the same process I explained in the TweetDeck registration process. Figure 8–9, shows the most popular social networks to add to your account.

If you want to add Foursquare, Ping.fm, WordPress, MySpace, or Mixi to your HootSuite dashboard, click on Add a different social network. As you see, HootSuite lets you monitor and engage with many social networks from one dashboard.

HootSuite will take you through the process of authorizing the various social media applications with your social media accounts. Figure 8–10 shows the initial screen of the Twitter authorization process.

FIGURE 8–10. Authorizing HootSuite to Access Your Twitter Account

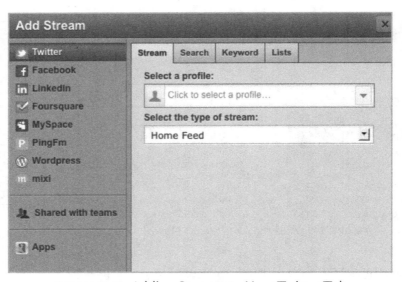

FIGURE 8–11. Adding Streams to Your Twitter Tab

This process connects your Twitter account with your HootSuite account so you can perform all of your Twitter functions from within your HootSuite dashboard. The authorization process is identical to the process I described in the TweetDeck signup process, so I don't need to walk you through it again. Simply let the signup wizard guide you through the process and everything will work fine.

Once your Twitter and HootSuite accounts are authorized to work together, you will be automatically added to your HootSuite Team as an Advanced Member. You have full permission to monitor and Tweet from your Twitter account, just like you were logged into your account at www.twitter.com.

Your next step is to add Streams to your Twitter tab as you see in Figure 8–11.

Click on the Add Stream button and HootSuite will walk you through the process of adding Streams to your tab. You will have a choice of four types of Streams to add to your first tab:

- Profile Stream
- Search
- Keyword
- Lists

Profile Stream

The Profile Stream lets you monitor specific types of activity that are part of your Twitter stream. Figure 8–12, page 129, shows the different activities you can monitor in

FIGURE 8–12. Adding Profile Streams to Your HootSuite Dashboard

your stream. I like to monitor my Home Feed, Mentions, Direct Message (Inbox), and my Scheduled Tweets. There are activities that I may have to respond to in a timely manner. I monitor my Favorite Tweets, ReTweets to me, and My Tweets, ReTweeted in my Analytics reports because I don't need to respond to them in a timely manner. You can choose which types of Streams you want to add to your dashboard. If your dashboard gets too cluttered, it's easy to remove the stream by clicking on the small downward-pointing triangle in the top right corner of the column and selecting Delete Stream.

Search Stream

The next type of Stream is the Search Stream, which is similar to a keyword search you would do on Google. You can enter some very specific search terms to be displayed in your Stream. Figure 8–13, page 130, shows you some examples of the search queries you can perform and monitor in your Stream. This is very helpful when you are monitoring specific hashtags you are using for events or promotional campaigns. You can also monitor your competitor's brand name and their product names to see which are most popular.

There are many search operators you can use to fine-tune your Twitter search results, so play around with a few and see which ones work best for your needs. You can see the

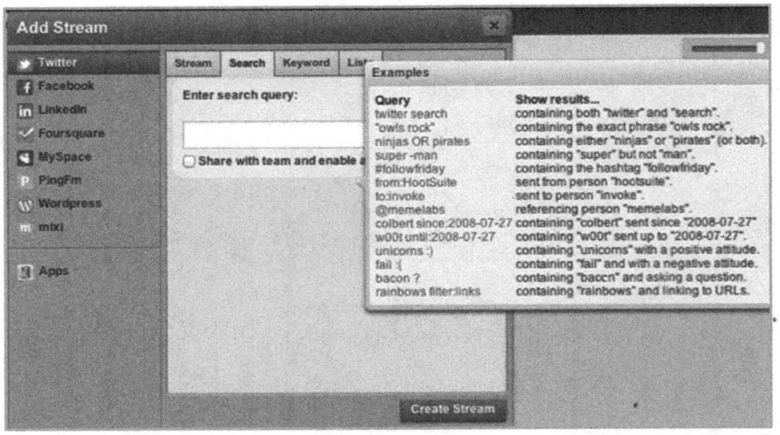

FIGURE 8–13. Adding Search Queries as a Stream

example search queries by clicking on the Search tab under Add Stream, then clicking on Show Examples. You can also share your Search Stream with your team members if you have multiple people managing your social media. Each search query can be assigned to a specific team member so they can respond accordingly.

Keyword Stream

The Keyword stream is similar to the Search stream except you can enter up to three keywords or keyword phrases instead of just one in the Search stream. Let's say I wanted to monitor Twitter for Best Buy specials or deals. I can enter up to three keyword phrases, as shown in Figure 8-14, page 131. Whenever one of these keyword phrases shows up in Twitter, it will appear in my Stream.

Another great feature of the Keyword Stream is that you can archive the Tweets if you only enter one keyword phrase. You can enter your company Twitter hashtag or Twitter name and archive all of the Tweets that contain your brand name. This is very helpful because Twitter does not archive all Tweets because of the extreme volume of Tweets every day. You can also share your Keyword Stream with your Team and assign specific Keyword Streams to each Team member.

Lists

Last but not least, you can create and monitor your Twitter Lists from your HootSuite dashboard. You learned about the power of Twitter Lists in Chapter 7; now I'll show you how to add Lists to your HootSuite Stream. As you see in Figure 8-15, page 131, you can create and monitor Lists for each Twitter profile you have. This is very handy if your company has multiple team members managing your social media activity.

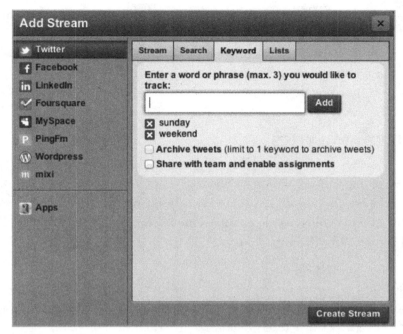

FIGURE 8–14. Setting Up Keyword Streams to Monitor for Specific Keyword Phrases

FIGURE 8–15. Monitoring and Creating Twitter Lists from Your Stream

You can add Lists that you create and Lists that you are subscribed to in this Stream. Twitter Lists are very similar to email distribution lists; you can contact numerous Twitter users at once instead of reaching out to them one at a time. When you subscribe to a Twitter List you can communicate with everyone on the List and you will receive all of the Tweets from everyone on that List.

HOOTSUITE ANALYTICS

HootSuite Analytics is a very powerful reporting tool that provides over 30 standard reporting modules and the ability to create custom reports. You can create detailed reports that are reserved for social media monitoring tools that cost thousands of dollars per month, but you're only paying $9.99 per month for the Pro level of HootSuite. You don't find bargains like this very often.

Quick Analytics

HootSuite comes with four prebuilt reports and the ability to create custom reports in the Quick Analytics tab. The four prebuilt reports are shown in Figure 8–16.

Ow.ly Summary Stats

This is a summary of the Ow.ly links you added to your Tweets. This report shows you how many clicks there were on each link and the number of clicks per day during a date range you specify for the report. Figure 8–17 on page 133 shows you the "Summary Stats" report.

As you see, this quick report provides a lot of detail. You not only see the quantity of clicks, but also what country the clicks are coming from, the referrer of the clicks, and your most popular links. This is a great way for you to see what type of content and the

FIGURE 8–16. Quick Analytics Reports

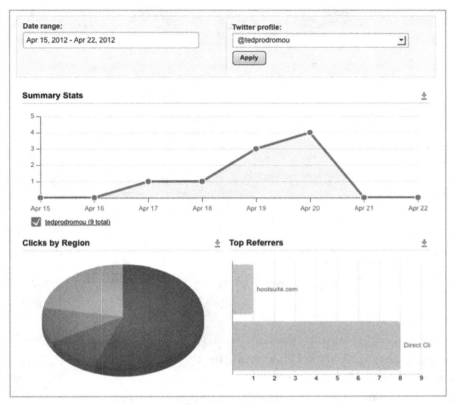

FIGURE 8–17. The "Summary Stats" Report

topics your followers are interested in. As with all of the HootSuite Analytics reports, you have the option to export to PDF, CSV, and print or customize the report so you can share it with your clients or team members.

Ow.ly Individual URL Stats

This report gives you details about individual URLs that were Tweeted. It's a simple report, as you see in Figure 8–18, page 134, telling you how many clicks per day each URL received. Personally, I don't find this report very useful because it only tells me how many clicks per day each URL received and not where the clicks came from. Tweeted URLs have a very short life, so this chart will only span a day or two in most cases.

When I run the "Ow.ly Individual URL Stats" report, I customize it, and add modules such as "Mentions by Influencers," "Profile Summary," and "Sentiment" to learn more about who Mentioned or ReTweeted the Tweet. If the Tweet was only ReTweeted a few times but it was by some influential Twitter users, I consider it a successful Tweet.

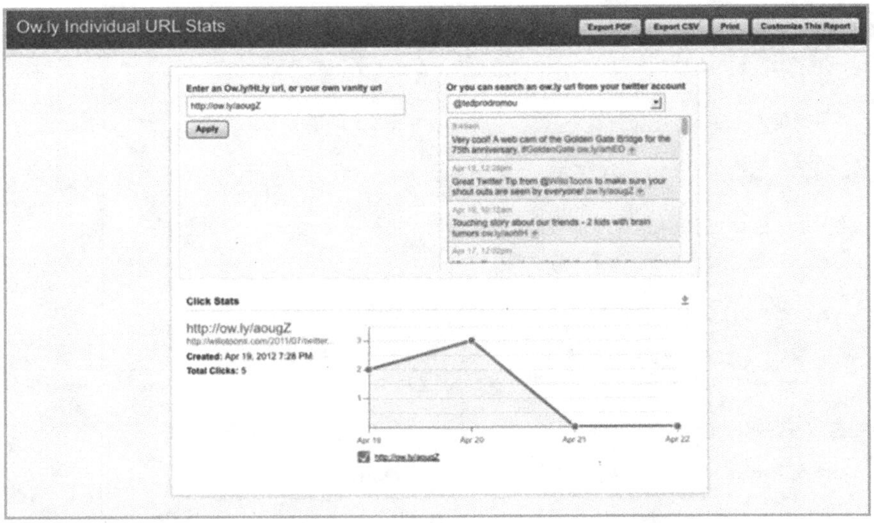

FIGURE 8–18. The Ow.ly Individual URL Stats Report

Facebook Insights

The integration of HootSuite Analytics with Facebook Insights gives you valuable information about your Twitter followers and Facebook Fans (see Figure 8–19). Everyone should have a Facebook Fan Page for their company. With almost 1 billion members, Facebook is the dominant social media platform. You need to be engaging your prospects and customers on every major social media platform. Being able to track their

FIGURE 8–19. Facebook Insights

activity on every platform using HootSuite Analytics will help you identify what they are interested in so you can create products and services they are looking for.

Knowing what content your Facebook Fans like gives you the information you need to create similar content to keep them interested in your company. Competition is fierce, so you have to constantly have your finger on your prospects' and customers' pulse. Facebook is a great tool to help you connect with your fans on a business level as well as a personal level. You have to constantly give them what they're looking for, then use Twitter to let them know where to find it.

Google Analytics

You also have the ability to import your Google Analytics data into your HootSuite Analytics reports. This lets you see the web traffic generated by each Tweet and the actions they took on your website, as you see in Figure 8–20. You should always Tweet a call to action with a link to your website, where your followers can complete that action. Twitter is a great tool for grabbing someone's attention and giving them a solution to their problem, which could be in the form of a white paper, video embedded on your website, or a blog post. When you Tweet a link to your website, that asset should be on its own landing page so you can track the performance of each Tweet and see which ones interest your followers. This lets you create new products and services that fulfill their needs.

FIGURE 8–20. Google Analytics Integration with HootSuite Analytics

You also see which countries and cities respond to your Tweets as well as all of the demographic information captured by Google Analytics. Knowing the detailed demographics of who's responding to your Tweets and the content they are interested in is probably the most important marketing information you can obtain. And it's almost free with your HootSuite Pro account.

We've only scratched the surface of what you can do with HootSuite. It's a very powerful dashboard that lets you manage many of your social media accounts from one screen. They're constantly adding new social media sites and tools to the dashboard, so it's worth taking a look at.

Price: Free for Basic version, $9.99 a month for Pro version, and the Enterprise version is $1,499 per month.

The Free version gives you:
- Five free quick reports
- Five social profiles
- Two RSS feeds
- Ads are displayed on your dashboard

The Pro version gives you:
- Unlimited social profiles
- One free additional team member; additional team members are $15.99 per month
- One free enhanced analytics report
- Google Analytics integration
- Facebook Insights integration
- Opt out of ads
- Archive Tweets
- Influence scores
- URL parameters
- App directory

The Enterprise version gives you:
- Unlimited social profiles
- Ten free reports
- Unlimited team members
- Unlimited RSS feeds
- Enhanced Analytics
- Ow.ly Pro Enterprise Vanity URL Ready—you get your own custom URL for shortened URL's

- Tier 1 Enterprise Support
- VIP Setup
- Opt out of ads
- Archive Tweets
- Certification program for 10 seats
- And more

Platforms: Web access via any browser, apps for iPhone, iPad, BlackBerry, and Android devices

SOCIALBRO

I recently came across SocialBro and was pleasantly surprised by the power of this free application. SocialBro's tagline is "browse your Twitter community," but that is a major understatement. This application does so much more than just browse your community. SocialBro lets you gain deep insight into your followers like no other free application available. SocialBro not only gives you in-depth analytical information about your Twitter followers, it makes it easy to communicate with them.

To get started, you can install the Chrome app and run SocialBro from your browser, or you can download the desktop app for Windows, Mac, and Linux. This is the only social media app I've seen that runs on any platform. The only downside I see is that it only works on desktop computers and isn't available for mobile devices at this time.

Some of the features available in SocialBro include:

- Browse your community
- Backup your community
- Manage your Twitter Lists
- Follow/Unfollow back tools
- Fast communication with your followers
- Search, filter, and sort all of Twitter
- Analytics scorecard of your community
- Observe the progress of your community
- See the evolution of your number of followers
- See the evolution of your number of friends
- See the evolution of your number of Tweets
- Manage your account step by step
- See your community as a map
- See your community in charts with numerous filters

■ Learn the best time to Tweet to your followers

■ Tag clouds let you see what your community is talking about

The SocialBro Dashboard

When you log into SocialBro, you're redirected to your dashboard, where you see a snapshot of your community. By default, everything is enabled on your dashboard, including Global Stats, your Tools bar, New Followers, Influence Stats, Recent Unfollows, and more. Each stat is contained in its own widget for easy viewing. If you are overwhelmed with the data displayed, you can delete or rearrange the widgets so the data you want to see is above the fold of your webpage or within the desktop application. Figure 8–21 shows your SocialBro dashboard in the default configuration. The screen scrolls down, displaying numerous widgets of Twitter data.

The lower half of your SocialBro dashboard displays your Twitter data in easy-to-read blocks or widgets. You can delete widgets by clicking on the [X] in the top right corner of the widget. You can move the widget by grabbing the top left corner of the widget and moving it to your desired data. This lets you display your important Twitter data near the top of your dashboard and your less important data at the bottom of the screen. See Figure 8–22 on page 139.

When you want to drill deeper to learn more about an influential Tweeter or a new follower, you just click on the images in the widget and a new window pops up with

FIGURE 8–21. Your SocialBro Dashboard

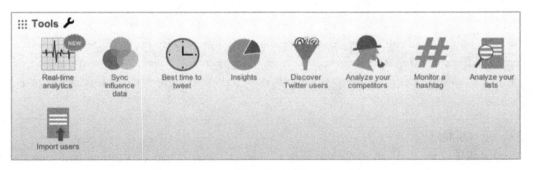

FIGURE 8–22. Twitter Data Is Organized in Easy-to-Configure Widgets

detailed profile information. SocialBro couldn't be easier to use and provides more data than most Twitter users need.

Tools

I like to call this the Tool Bar because it's your access to the analytics tools in SocialBro. As you see in Figure 8–23, you can dig deep into your Twitter data to see trends.

Real-Time Analytics

This tool lets you get a snapshot of what's happening in your Twitterverse right now. You see how many of your followers are online right now, the top languages, the top

FIGURE 8–23. The SocialBro Tool Bar

Twitter apps and clients, and how many users are active per second. When you see one of your followers online, you can engage them by clicking on their avatar, which pops open a window on the sidebar. From the sidebar you can view their profile in detail, send a Tweet to them, reply to one of their Tweets, ReTweet one of their Tweets, or Direct Message them. You can also add them to a list, unfollow them, or even block them if they turn out to be a bot or spammer.

Sync Influence Data
The next tool lets you sync the influence data from Twitter with your local database in SocialBro. The ability to sync your Twitter account with a local database lets you analyze and filter your Twitterverse data faster and also lets you keep your Twitter data forever. Because of the high volume of Tweets and interactions, Twitter.com is unable to keep historical data for more than a few days. You used to be able to look at all of your past Tweets and interactions, but it's now limited to a few days or the past 2,500 Tweets.

Best Time to Tweet
This is one of my favorite features of SocialBro. When you click on the Best Time to Tweet tool, SocialBro analyzes your Twitter followers and determines when it's best for you to Tweet based on their online habits. If you are using the free version of SocialBro, it will only analyze your top 100 followers, which still gives you a lot of very valuable information. Knowing when to reach your top 100 followers is great information to have.

Insights
The Insights tool breaks down your followers by language, time zone, avatar type, profiles with web URLs, and verified users. You also see the users by influence rank, number of followers, friends/followers ratio, time since last Tweet, Tweets per day, and my favorite, users by location, as shown in Figure 8–24, page 141.

Knowing where your followers are helps you create targeted marketing campaigns for each region. You can create one marketing campaign targeted toward North America and a different campaign targeted at your European followers. Your response rates will increase dramatically when you create targeted campaigns based on your follower location.

Discover Twitter Users
This tool is essentially the Discover tab in Twitter, which you can use to find people to follow. The advantage of the SocialBro version of this tool is that you can filter the

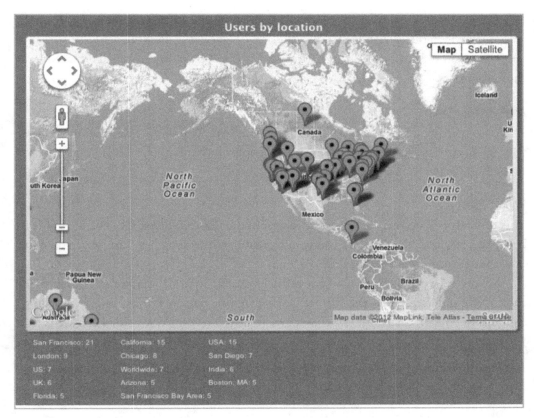

FIGURE 8–24. Twitter Followers by Location Lets You See Where Your Followers Are

recommended followers by number of followers (celebs dominate this), number of friends, Tweets, Tweets per day, date last Tweet, date added, or influence. This lets you find the best people to follow based on their Twitter activity and influence.

Analyze Your Competitors

I don't know of any other Twitter tool that does this so easily. Just enter the Twitter handle of your competitors and SocialBro imports all of their followers and Friends into your database. You can sort and filter their followers to see whom they are connected with. This is great business intelligence information you can use to see who their prospects and customers are.

Monitor a Hashtag

This tool is equivalent to a Twitter search. You can monitor for specific keywords or hashtags based on a Twitter Search, Twitter Account, your Twitter lists, other Twitter lists, or you can upload a text file.

The Monitor a Hashtag tool gives you the same results as you see when you add columns in TweetDeck and HootSuite.

When you monitor a hashtag, your dashboard will only display results that contain the keywords you specified.

Analyze Your Lists

This tool helps you filter your dashboard by your lists. You select one of your lists, and your dashboard only displays data from the people on that list. This helps you see which lists are most active and which are performing best.

Import Users

This tool lets you upload a list of users into your database via a text file. The file needs to be a plain text file, like the ones you would create with Notepad in Windows. You enter one Twitter user per line in the file.

As you see, SocialBro is a very powerful Twitter analytics and account management tool. We've only scratched the surface with what you can do with it, so I invite you to sign up for your free account today and give it a try. The only downside I can see is that you can't easily display your Twitter feed so you can see your Twitter Stream in real time.

Price: Premium $6.95/month; Professional $39/month; Business $149/month

Platforms: Social Desktop for Chrome browsers or Socialbro for Desktop which runs on Linux, Windows, or Apple IOS.

TWOPCHARTS

Twopcharts is one of the most comprehensive Twitter tools available today. As you see in Figure 8–25 on page 143, Twopcharts provides almost every Twitter statistic available today. Some of the most valuable Twitter statistics I monitor are Who Mentions Me, Must Follow, and My Top Followers. I like to see who is mentioning me in their Tweets and who my top followers are. I make a habit of thanking my followers for ReTweets, Mentions, and Replies. I also want to know who Twopcharts thinks I should be following. I'm always looking for new people to follow and I love the fact that Twopcharts helps identify potential people. I don't always agree with their suggestions, but it's a good starting point.

I also love the ability to select specific cities and languages, because the company I work for has offices around the world. I'm always looking for influential people in every country and in different languages so our local marketing teams can reach out to them.

Price: Free

Platforms: Browser-based

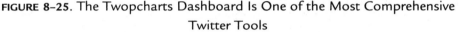

FIGURE 8–25. The Twopcharts Dashboard Is One of the Most Comprehensive Twitter Tools

TWEETBOT

When I first downloaded Tweetbot for iPhone, I thought it looked like most Twitter apps. I didn't understand why everyone was raving about this app. As you see in Figure 8–26 on page 144, Tweetbot looks like just another Twitter app.

Once you start playing with Tweetbot you'll see why it's one of the hottest Twitter apps on the market. Tweetbot is full of tapping and swiping shortcuts that make it easier to use than most Twitter apps. Some of the features of Tweetbot include:

Multiple Timelines

Tweetbot lets you use your Twitter Lists as fully functional timelines so you can filter your Twitter Stream. If you only want to see Tweets from friends, you select your friend list on the timeline. If you only want to see Tweets from your competitors, select your competitors list on the timeline. A simple swipe is all it takes to change timelines so you can check your Twitter Lists.

Conversations and Replies

Tweetbot lets you easily monitor Twitter conversations and replies. Just swipe to the right on a conversation and you see the entire conversation thread. When you swipe to

FIGURE 8–26. The Tweetbot App for the iPhone

the left, you see all of the replies to a conversation. You don't even have to be the author of the conversation to see the entire conversation and replies.

Smart Gestures

Tweetbot has smart gestures that can save you time.

- Tap a link or avatar in your timeline to view more so you can reply, ReTweet, or mark as a favorite.
- Double-tapping a Tweet takes you to the Tweet detail.
- Tap on the avatar accompanying a Tweet to go directly to that user's profile. Tap and hold on the avatar, and you'll get options to send that user a direct message,

manage which Twitter Lists you put that user on, mute the user, or Unfollow that person, as shown in Figure 8–27.

■ And finally you can configure triple-tap to Reply-to, Fave, ReTweet, or even translate a Tweet.

Similarly, single-tapping a Tweet brings up buttons for common actions like replying, ReTweeting, or marking as a favorite; tapping and holding it instead brings up options to save an embedded link (to services like Instapaper and Read It Later), copy a link to the Tweet, copy the text of the Tweet, email the Tweet, or translate it.

Customizable Tab Bar

You can customize the last two tabs in Tweetbot. Just hold down the tab for a split second and change it to a new selection.

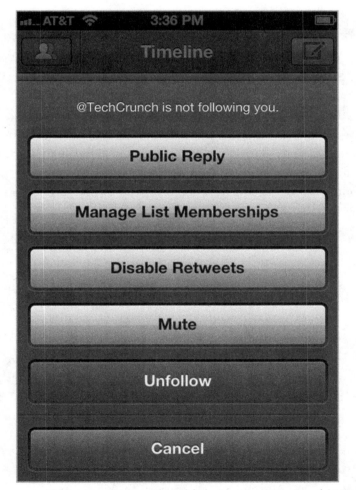

FIGURE 8–27. When You Tap and Hold the Avatar You See this Screen

Integration with Other Services

Tweetbot is integrated with services like Readability, Google Mobilizer, and Instapaper for presenting easier-to-read versions of web pages you visit. These services streamline the web content so it's easier to read on your mobile device.

Tweetbot is also integrated with Tweet Marker, which syncs your last-read Tweet between multiple apps and devices. This lets you start reading on one device and continue reading on a different device that's running Tweet Marker.

Tweetbot is easy to learn, and feature rich. It's one of the best mobile apps for Twitter.

Price: $2.99

Platforms: iPhone and iPad only

INSTAGRAM

Instagram is a photo-sharing app that made big news in April 2012 when Facebook acquired it for $1 billion. Not bad for a two-year-old startup with 14 employees and no revenue!

Snap a picture with your iPhone, apply a digital filter to enhance the photo if you want, and you can upload the picture to Facebook, Twitter, and Flickr. You can also upload pictures directly to your Tumblr blog and your Foursquare account. Instagram photos are different than other digital photos because they resemble Polaroid or Kodak Instamatic photos, which are square in shape instead of the 4:3 ratio of normal digital photos.

Price: Free

Platform: iPhone only

BUFFER

Buffer is a new application that lets you schedule your social media posts on Twitter, Facebook, or LinkedIn. You can also integrate Buffer with other apps to schedule updates in SocialBro, Twylah, Tweetings, Digg, Tweroid, and many other popular apps. The initial reviews for Buffer have been exceptional, and it's one of the fastest-growing social media apps available. Buffer is very easy to use and the integration with the other social media apps and sites is seamless.

Price: Free

Platform: iPhone and Android, plus extensions for Firefox and Chrome.

TWEETCHAT

TweetChat is a free tool that lets you create easy-to-follow Twitter chats in real time. TweetChats are becoming a popular marketing tool for companies. A TweetChat is essentially a live panel discussion that is held on Twitter. You assign a moderator to the TweetChat to ask questions and to keep the conversation flowing. Expert panelists take turns discussing the questions and debating their answers.

TweetChat is very easy to use, as you see in Figure 8–28. You assign a hashtag to your TweetChat and promote it using your normal marketing channels, including Twitter. Each panelist logs into TweetChat and follows the hashtag. As questions appear, they respond accordingly. The entire conversation is tagged with your hashtag so the TweetChat is easy for your prospects and customers to follow.

Price: Free

Platforms: Any web browser on PC or Mac.

TWITPIC

This section would not be complete without Twitpic, because it was one of the first photo-sharing apps for Twitter. When you take a picture with your smartphone, you can easily upload the picture to your Twitpic page and automatically send a Tweet with

FIGURE 8–28. TweetChat Is an Easy-to-Use Tool to Facilitate Online Discussions

a link to the photo. Twitpic also lets you create Events so your attendees can all post pictures from the event on your Twitpic event page.

You can also add a widget to your blog or website so your Twitpic pictures will automatically appear on your sites. Twitpic is one of the original Twitter apps and has always been easy to set up and use. There are lots of other picture apps for Twitter, but Twitpic is still one of my favorites.

Price: Free

Platform: TwitPic is an app that runs on Apple IOS or Android.

COTWEET

CoTweet is another powerful social media management tool that is designed for businesses and enterprises. ExactTarget, an online marketing solutions company, recently acquired CoTweet, which calls itself a "Social CRM" because its primary feature is a workflow option that lets teams coordinate the management of their social media. See Figure 8–29.

CoTweet lets you assign team members to specific Tweets so they can respond with the appropriate expertise. CoTweet sends out email notifications whenever a message is assigned to a team member or when the assignment is completed. CoTweet helps you track and coordinate your social media activity within large companies.

FIGURE 8–29. CoTweet Is a Social Media Management Dashboard for Teams

Price: Standard version is free. Enterprise version starts from $1,500/month.

Platform: Browser-based

REFOLLOW

Refollow is a handy tool that helps you manage your Twitter network. You can see who's following you, their profile details, including how many Tweets they do and how many people they follow, and even when they sent their last Tweet. The Refollow dashboard is easy to use and lets you select from an array of search criteria. Figure 8–30 shows you the Refollow dashboard.

Refollow also helps you easily set up and manage your Twitter Lists. You can use the search criteria to find new people to follow and add to each List.

TWYLAH

Many Twitter management tools perform similar functions, such as displaying

FIGURE 8–30. The Refollow Dashboard Lets You Easily Manage Your Twitter Network

important Twitter statistics, scheduling Tweets, uploading pictures, or helping you easily share social media content. Twylah is a different breed of Twitter application. Twylah will take your Twitter content and turn it into a beautiful web page. The average Tweet lives about one hour. When you turn your Tweets into web pages with Twylah, the life of your Tweet is extended indefinitely. You can even host your Twylah content on your own domain name so you extend your brand. Figure 8–31 shows Bon Jovi's branded Twylah page.

Twylah exists to drive deeper engagement with your Twitter followers. Many times your Tweets go unread and disappear quickly if they aren't ReTweeted or Mentioned.

FIGURE 8–31. Bon Jovi's Twylah Page with Links to iTunes and His iPhone App

Posting your Twitter content on your Twylah page will allow your content to be discovered through other web channels like Google search. Once users find your content on your Twylah page, they can easily read and respond to your Tweet. Twylah adds a whole new dimension to your Tweets.

Price: Free (you have to request an invite)

Platform: Browser-based

CONCLUSION

There are many other Twitter tools available and more are being developed every day as Twitter evolves. These are the tools I currently use, and I'm constantly testing new ones as they're released. I encourage you to take some time and try these tools because they will help you use Twitter more effectively.

In the next chapter, you're going to meet some people who have used Twitter to transform their businesses. These people are not social media celebrities. They're small-business owners, just like you and I, who embraced Twitter and use it daily to successfully promote and grow their businesses.

Twitter Success Stories

Every day businesses are finding new ways to use Twitter to spread the word about new promotions, build their brand, and build strong relationships with their customers. There are hundreds, if not thousands, of Twitter success stories I could share with you. Many big brands have figured out how to use Twitter to enhance advertising campaigns, with some campaigns even centering around Twitter.

In case you aren't familiar with the brands who "get" Twitter, I recommend following companies like Dominos, Comcast, Zappos, Dell Computers, Starbucks, Network Solutions, Computer Associates, Volkswagen, and Ben & Jerry's. There are many other big brands that use Twitter effectively, and I recommend following those who do it well so you can learn from their successful marketing campaigns.

Dominos uses Twitter to build their brand and to gather valuable feedback from their customers. Most of you have probably heard how Comcast started monitoring Twitter a few years ago so they could respond to dissatisfied customers. @ComcastCares turns out to be one of the biggest Twitter success stories ever. Check out the other companies I mentioned and search Google for "Twitter success stories" to see how other brands are using Twitter to their advantage.

Instead of focusing on big brands and Twitter power users like @ChrisBrogan, @GuyKawasaki, or @LadyGaga, I'm going to introduce you to five small-business owners who've used Twitter to grow their businesses and built strong relationships with their customers. These Twitter users are just like you; they own successful small businesses without having millions of Twitter followers.

These people have a lot in common with each other and with many Twitter power users. There are a few common traits that all successful Twitter users have, including:

- Authenticity
- Listening more than Tweeting
- Showing gratitude
- Constantly promoting others by ReTweeting, replying to, and mentioning others
- Providing useful information to their followers
- Refraining from self-promoting
- Participating actively on Twitter at least three to five times a day

I haven't met all of these people in person, but I feel like I've known all of them forever, and they are good friends. Let me introduce you to Susan RoAne, Mark Guinnebaugh, Carrie Wilkerson, Eric Jan van Putten, and Michelle Bucher and let them share how they successfully use Twitter to promote their businesses.

SUSAN ROANE @SUSANROANE

I'm a very shy person by nature and I used to hate going to networking events. I wasn't comfortable trying to strike up a conversation with a complete stranger. I would hang out on the side of the room and hope nobody would approach me. I know it sounds strange to attend a networking event and hope nobody would talk to me, but I was that uncomfortable. Then I read a book in 1990 called *How to Work a Room* by Susan RoAne that changed my life.

How to Work a Room taught me how to get over my fear of people and how to feel comfortable around strangers. Today I love going to networking events and meeting new people. *How to Work a Room* not only taught me how to network effectively, it helped me get over my fear of speaking in public. Once I felt comfortable speaking one-on-one with others, I wanted to conquer my fear of speaking in front of groups. They say people are more afraid of speaking in public than they are of dying. That's a powerful statement, and reading *How to Work a Room* helped me conquer a lot of my fears.

A couple of years ago I was giving a presentation about Twitter at a local networking event. Twitter was a hot topic so we had a larger than normal crowd, which invigorated rather than intimidated me. Before my talk, everyone was networking with each other and I started talking with a woman. She told me she was an author and had written *How to Work a Room*. I was so excited to meet Susan RoAne in person and was honored that she was attending my Twitter presentation. I told her my story about reading her book over 20 years earlier and how it had changed my life. We instantly bonded and became best friends. We get together for lunch often and communicate regularly on Twitter, ReTweeting and Replying to each other's Tweets.

Business name: The RoAne Group

Website/blog: www.susanroane.com

Joined Twitter: 2008

Followers: 1,421

Following: 488

Tweets: 4,022

Susan RoAne leads a double life as a bestselling author and a sought-after professional keynote speaker. Known as The Mingling Maven®, she gives diverse audiences the required tools, techniques, and strategies they need to connect and communicate in today's global business world. Her practical, informative, and interactive presentations are known for what *The San Francisco Chronicle* calls her "dynamite sense of humor."

RoAne's audiences learn How to Work a Room® and master the art of face-to-face communication in any setting. With her timeless tips, anyone can overcome shyness and learn to schmooze with confidence in business networking or social gatherings. Some of the organizations that have hired Susan as a professional keynote speaker are: AT&T, Apple, Coca-Cola, Kraft Foods, Time Warner, Office Depot, Boeing, Citigroup, Ernst and Young, United States Department of The Treasury, Oracle, Procter and Gamble, United States Air Force, National Football League and, her personal favorite, Hershey's Chocolate.

Because of her groundbreaking bestseller, *How to Work a Room*, SusanRoAne is considered one of the most influential networking and business communication experts. She has sold over a million books worldwide, and helped launch an industry that she continues to recreate and shape today.

Susan RoAne received her master's degree from San Francisco State University and her bachelor's from the University of Illinois Champaign-Urbana, where she was honored at "Authors Come Home." (She still considers herself a Fighting Illini!) A former teacher, Susan is also a sought-after college keynote speaker at major universities such as Yale, Wharton, University of Chicago, Regent University, and NYU.

A resident of the beautiful San Francisco Bay Area, Susan is a member of The National Speakers Association, The Authors Guild, the MS society, a supporter of The Mill Valley Film Festival, as well as a Friend of the San Francisco Ballet.

TED: When and why did you join Twitter?

SUSAN: [In] July, 2008, I'd written about it and knew of it from reading our San Francisco newspapers.

TED: How long did it take you to do your first Tweet, and do you remember what it was?

SUSAN: Fairly quickly, because it's part of my business branding. I can't remember the exact date I first Tweeted. I can't remember my first Tweet.

TED: What tips do you have for someone who doesn't know what to say on Twitter, and how many times do you Tweet per day or week?

SUSAN: I personally read the newspapers, magazines and share breaking news or interesting articles that would contribute to others. Generally, [I Tweet] three times a day depending on how many interesting articles I read or the current news events of the day.

TED: What are your favorite Twitter tools, and how do you use Twitter for business?

SUSAN: I use SocialOomph and HootSuite. I used to love and use Twaitter and I hated my switch to Gremln. I share that for which I am known . . . via my books and speaking. I also like to share interesting comments, funny or poignant quotes with my followers.

TED: Do you use Twitter to research trends or your competitors? What impact has Twitter had on your business?

SUSAN: Rarely do I use Twitter to do research . . . but I do use it to check on me! . . . I use it to reinforce my brand as the original networking authority, including the schmoozing with others. I use Twitter to promote ideas and other people's books as well as constantly provide socializing Twitter tips to help others.

TED: What impact has Twitter had on your personal life, if any?

SUSAN: I've met new people like Jeremiah Owyang and Tamar Weinberg . . . two social media gurus. I also met Peter Cashmore (Mashable) and have touched base with many colleagues, clients, and potential clients.

TED: What tips do you have for someone just getting started on Twitter?

SUSAN:	Always be of value. DON'T ever write anything you wouldn't want to defend in a court of law.
TED:	Who are your favorite people you follow?
SUSAN:	Jon Stewart, Jeremiah Owyang, HilzFuld, Mashable, TechCrunch, TheTweetOFGod (totally hysterical), MikeMuhney (founder of Act! and VIPOrbit), so many SMART people. I also follow my two grandsons to keep up with them.
TED:	What is your favorite Twitter story? (My favorite Twitter story is that I met one of my favorite authors because she came to a presentation I was doing about Twitter.)
SUSAN:	Love you for that! Meeting you is one of them, and three years later I was asked to do a presentation on how to use Twitter.
	At a Giants vs. Cubs game, I stayed to finish a Tweet after the Giants won. Only two other guys with computers were sitting in their box seats. On my way out I made an off-the-cuff remark and they swore they were "working."
	"Really, where do you work, in the right field box seats?"
	"Twitter," they responded.
	"No kidding! That's why I stayed late, to finish a Tweet on my iPad." They checked me out, saw I was Tweeting through the game and "Favorited" my Tweets.
TED:	What else do you have to say about Twitter?
SUSAN:	Twitter has made me a better self-editor and consumer of the four newspapers I read, because I always read with an eye for "will this be useful, informative, fun" for my followers and help them make conversation.
	I do all my own Tweeting . . . . Most paid social media people may capture the info but rarely make the Tweets have the element of personality that engages.
TED:	What are some of the biggest mistakes people make when they are networking, whether it's online or offline?
SUSAN:	One of the most irritating questions I hear at networking events is the person who comes up and says, "What can I do to support you?" I don't even know you, who are you? What do you mean, "What can you do to support me?" How about, "Let's have a conversation, find out a little bit about each other,

maybe share some information—if we're lucky, a laugh." Because to me, the instance of *what can I do to support you* has an air of self-congratulatory conceit. I am so important I can support you—really? How do we know that? We know these things through conversation. We are forgetting the dating part of it, the getting to know you. Right away you want to jump into a marriage. It's untimely, it's unseemly, and most often it doesn't work because really, what am I going to say to you? "You know what? If you could get me three speaking engagements a month within 50 miles of home, that's what I need. And by the way, if I don't have to wear pantyhose when I speak, that would make it even nicer."

TED: So how do you get to the dating stage on Twitter so you can build that relationship?

SUSAN: The dating stage on Twitter is when you see something that someone sends and you respond to it in some way. Now here's my pet peeve on Twitter: People who block messages. A couple years ago I saw a nice Tweet about me so I wanted to reach out and thank him. When I tried to contact him on Twitter, he was blocking all messages from everyone. My first thought was, "What? You're blocking me?" You've got two followers and you're blocking messages. How dumb is that? So what I did is I found his email and I said, "I am so appreciative of what you said to me and I wanted to send you a direct message but for some reason you have blocked messages, so I couldn't get this to you. You might want to consider unblocking people." When my guru—who I adore, Jeremiah Owyang, now of the Altimeter Group—doesn't block his direct messages, who in the hell are the rest of these people blocking *their* messages? I just don't block the messages, because to me I think if you have a million followers that may be legitimate, but I know that people use their lists. How are you supposed to build relationships with others if you block their messages?

TED: I remember a story you told me about the early days of online networking, when people used to meet online and offline. Can you share that story?

SUSAN: About 15 years ago there used to be a website called The Well, where people would meet online. It was one of the original groups where people with common interests connected online. There was a chat group and everyone wanted to meet each other because they had formed such good connections online. There was a group of children's authors and they had a big online forum. Eventually they followed each other on Twitter and then one of the women Tweeted, "Gee, if we would have had a potluck while we were together, what would you bring?" Oh my gosh, people went, "Oh, what would I bring?" The Twitter stream went crazy. They finally decided that they had to have a conference and they all met in Chicago. People flew in from all over, and they said things like, "Oh, you look just like I expected you to," because they all kind of knew each other but not really. People felt like they knew each other for years. And it was called "Kiddy-Lit," short for kid's literature.

TED: What do you share on Twitter for fun?

SUSAN: Twitter is a wonderful way to stay in touch and it's a wonderful way, as far as I'm concerned, of sharing something of value that isn't by you. It's not like I share a lot of stuff about myself. Oh my gosh, I just wrote a blog for the shy brides, because I've always talked to bridal magazines. So I wrote a blog about shy brides, and I Tweeted it. Then I also Tweeted about "This is a great book," or "This is a movie you'll really enjoy." Oh . . . I know what one of my Tweets was, oh my God—the best Saturday Night Live, who knew (now I am just going to forget his name . . . Rolling Stone)—

TED: Was it Mick Jagger?

SUSAN: Yes! Who knew Mick Jagger had that much comedic timing? He was brilliant. Sometimes what I'll do is I'll send a link to the YouTube of it, if someone wants to watch. So what you do is you share, you support, which is what networking is. You ask questions, you pose food for thought . . . It's like having a great brainstorming session. You can ask, "Has anyone ever come up with this and how did you handle it?" And a group of people will expand on it and you might get your answer.

But I think it's always important to acknowledge and thank others. When someone says something nice about you, take a moment and thank them. You will break your arm patting yourself on the back if you ReTweet all the nice things people said about you.

TED: Good point, that's a really good point. People really appreciate it when you take time to thank them publicly for something they did for you.

SUSAN: I was just in the carnival, by the way. I went to the UC Med Center, my niece, not by blood but by love, graduated UC Medical School Monday. So I had my binoculars on the parents and the significant others of the doctors at the hood ceremony, which is a tender, touching ceremony. I'm looking in my binoculars and all of a sudden, it's like, "That's Kareem Abdul-Jabbar" and I had to see if my cataract was failing me, and there was Kareem Abdul-Jabbar in person. I looked on the program and his son graduated medical school and he was hooding his son. A couple minutes later, we get to the Cs and I see a Chinese lady with a white boy, kind of curly hair, he looked very familiar, but I wasn't sure who he was. He was wearing a nice blue sweater, beaming ear to ear, hooding his wife. At the end of the reception my friend Pam says "Oh my God, there's Zuckerman!" I said, "Zuckerman"? She said, "Zuckerman, you know, Zuckerman." I said, "What are you talking about?" She said "Facebook." I said, "Oh, Zuckerberg!" I watched him the whole time through the binoculars, beaming. On that Monday she was his fiancée, but by Saturday she was his wife and Facebook went public the same week.

TED: So did you Tweet about all this excitement at the ceremony?

SUSAN: I am sitting in the center in this ceremony and I right away Tweet—"Kareem Abdul-Jabbar just Tweeted about his son." I actually took a picture of him and Tweeted it, too. I Tweeted about seeing Mark Zuckerberg immediately and then after the ceremony, I went to Facebook and wrote, "In case you were wondering where Mark Zuckerberg is today, which happened to be his birthday, he's at the UCSF Med School where he just hooded his long-time girlfriend." And I wrote, "He wasn't wearing a hoody, he was wearing a smile." And it was nice for me to Tweet and post on Facebook, but I also wrote about it because people have to have context for who you are. I sent that item into the San Francisco Chronicle, too. The item appeared in the paper, and because I was such a good spy, Leah Garchick wrote, "Because Susan RoAne is such a good spy, I might mention she was there because her niece Nicole Whitell was also becoming a doctor." So really, what does online networking do? You have to still be your networker online and you still have to think of other people. You can promote yourself a little bit, but if all you do is promote yourself, it pisses people off.

TED: Do you feel like a reporter that reports the news via Twitter? You share a lot of great information on social media.

SUSAN: I report a lot of news via Twitter. I also congratulate and I also ReTweet. And if I have a comment I might put the Tweet in quotes and write my own not in quotes that says, *really cool*, *don't miss*, or *very valuable*. I once did a Tweet because they have this thing called the Mingle-Stick where you put—it's like you can do it now with smartphones—you put them together and they absorb each other's contact information, which I have always felt is dangerous. In fact, I wrote about it in my book, *Face to Face*, because the truth is, if you're just rubbing smartphones, how are you going to remember the person's name when it's time to follow up with them? So business cards are not going to go out of style. We'd like to think they are, but actually they are becoming more expensive. You can either get them for free, or have one that actually features you.

TED: People will remember you for the wrong reasons if you are just sharing contact information through your smartphone. You need to give them a reason to remember you and to keep in touch.

SUSAN: Yes, they remember you for the wrong reasons. Now this is why you have to have friends in different age groups. You have to have older friends so you know where to buy doilies, and then you have to have younger friends, like my friend Michael and his kids. I go over there every three months for dinner when I can and he says, "Do you have a QR code?" I said, "No, what is a QR code?" Well, Michael used to work with me and help me on my computer. Now he works full time with some private clients, and he went and got me a QR code. Am I like the coolest person on my block because I have a QR code? It just so happens my QR code is now on my envelopes, it's on my handouts, and I'm trying to figure out how to get them on my business cards that I just had printed. I now Tweet an image of my QR code so people can download information from me.

TED: I know you keep in touch with a lot of old friends on Twitter. How do you communicate with your friends there?

SUSAN: That's the wonderful thing about Twitter. We want to stay in touch in different geographic locations and Twitter is a global community so it's easy to keep in touch. Twitter is also a generational community. Some of the biggest Tweeters might be 60 and others might be 26. So you have to have your eyes open to know you can learn. There is so much to learn from people of different ages. And I was kidding about the doilies, because if you see that I'm buying them, just shoot me! But to me, if you really pay attention to Twitter you can learn so much. I have been an author and a writer for a long time, since the *Examiner* career series in 1980, but I have been an author since 1988. Twitter has made me a better writer. Twitter has made me a better editor. It's also made me a better reader because I read four papers a day, three days a week, and three papers the other days of the week. And that's not even online. That's in addition to what I do online, and I always read with the idea of what can I find that would be of interest, would be funny, something someone might not know that would be ironic. I said there's two kinds of humor—ironic and moronic, I personally like to go with the ironic. I like to Tweet little things and little quotes. Sometimes I will listen to Jon Stewart or Steven Colbert and Tweet their funny lines. Nobody is a better writer than the writers of those shows. That's why there are so many little pieces of paper around my house that I could actually wallpaper the queen's castle with them. So always keep in mind when you hear things that are interesting, would they be good Tweets? Would they make someone smile? The Tweets don't always have to inform, educate, and promote. It's a way of staying in touch, like saying I thought of you or I wanted to share a smile.

TED: So you give people in your network a little ping once in a while to stay in touch. It doesn't take a lot of time but it's a way for you to tell them you are thinking about them.

SUSAN: A little ping, yeah, and it's a little reminder. Someone will say it costs 45 cents, and in what country for 45 cents can you do something nice for someone? And now I am going to get on my soap box. Some things still have to be retro. A young man who has redesigned my blog and has done all my videos posted on Facebook that his grandmother passed away. I sent a little Facebook note, then I found his address and sent him an email, too. I thought that is not a Susan RoAne thing, so I went to the store and bought him a sympathy card for his grandmother—it said grandma on it. It kind of makes me tear up, because here's this young man and what I found out is that mine was the only sympathy card he got. He got sympathy emails, he got sympathy comments on Facebook, but the difference is, in six months, in six weeks, in six years, one person took the time. When I knew that it wasn't just a grandma, it was the grandma that he lived with for ten years, I knew that this was significant. So I am going to say that while we embrace Twitter and we embrace social media, it's not even networking, it's having a heart. It's having empathy. I still have the sympathy cards, not only from when my mother died, but from when mumsy died, she was like better than a friend/mother to me. So I think we can do things online, but we shouldn't forget our offline behaviors. For me, I really enjoy Twitter. I have worked hard for each one of my followers. I sometimes forget to say, "Follow me," I sometimes forget to pitch things because I'm the ultimate teacher, so let me say one more thing you can do to fill up a room. Honestly, I think I have like 1,414 followers, but they are real people, they are not bots. Oh, the other thing I'd say about Twitter—maybe it was you, Ted, who taught me this, oh my God, it was you!—that having 7,000 followers if you follow 8,000 people doesn't really show much, so I have always been very cautious, I'm almost three to one. I am followed three times more than I follow. I didn't do it because there were Klout scores. I did it because when I made this decision, when we talked there was no Klout, and by the way Klout with a K is one thing, but if you really want to be important, you have clout with a C. Together it's nice, but really go for clout with a C, though I would say that and I again would even kind of challenge my own remarks, because I just read that some airlines look up your Klout score when you go to get your ticket, and if they see you have 40 or more points they might upgrade you.

TED: Oh my God. You're serious, aren't you? They really upgrade you based on your Klout score? I can't believe it.

SUSAN: So the schmoe that has more Klout than you and I together will be sitting in first class because he bought all his followers. I think you have to be smart. I think you have to have a strategy but the other thing is you just have to do it. If you're on Twitter and you're a lurker, there's a way that we can have you unfollow us, am I right?

TED: Yep. You're right. You can always unfollow someone if they aren't the right fit for your network.

SUSAN: So I did do that one day. Obviously this was a woman with too much time on her hands and no soap operas to watch. I sat at my computer, went through my followers, because I had some raunchy people start following me, I thought, "Ooh, I don't want"—and you know I swear, but I don't want someone who's got the F-bomb, etc., I don't know who's seeing it, I don't know any of that, I don't want that. So, I have to help people scoot away from me. Be careful what you Tweet . . . I know you said this in your book. You want to make sure that you don't put personal information [in your Tweets]. But the other part is, if every one of your Tweets is automated, you look like an ass . . . If it's Christmas and all you're sending is business Tweets, you look unprofessional. On Mother's Day I said, "Happy Mother's Day to those of you who are Moms and to those of us who celebrate with you." That was ReTweeted, and that was commented on, on Facebook. So if you are not doing your social media yourself, if something important happens and you have hired out all your Tweeting to other people, as if it's beneath you and you've hired this smart social media person, that there's nothing that says *oh my goodness today something cataclysmic and wonderful happened!*—then this shows me that all you're doing is self-promotion. So I would be very cautious, if you do hire someone, and even though they may capture your voice and read all your books and get all your little things, you've got to be a person on Twitter.

TED: That's great, that's perfect. Thank you so much for sharing your Twitter stories with me.

SUSAN: I really do mean that, about being a real person on Twitter. You need to Tweet yourself and be authentic. It's okay to automate some of your Tweets but you need to do the majority of your Tweeting.

MARK GINNEBAUGH @MARKGINNEBAUGH

I met Mark Ginnebaugh a few years ago at SofTECH, a local networking group that Mark runs in addition to many other software user groups in the San Francisco Bay Area. He and his wife Patti are frequent attendees of my Meetup group, the Bay Area Internet Marketers, where they learn the latest and greatest internet marketing tips.

Mark uses Twitter to promote his software user group events in the San Francisco Bay Area and to share relevant industry information with his followers. Interestingly, Mark doesn't use Twitter to promote his software development company DesignMind. I like Mark's natural approach to using Twitter because he engages in conversations, shares relevant articles and blog posts, and promotes his events very subtly. When you follow Mark on Twitter you get to know the real Mark Ginnebaugh because he's completely authentic both on Twitter and in real life. He's a genuinely nice person, which comes through loud and clear.

Business name: DesignMind

Website/blog: www.designmind.com

Joined Twitter: March 2009

Followers: 1,246

Following: 1,448

Number of Tweets: 2,807

Mark Ginnebaugh is president of DesignMind, a Microsoft Gold Partner that develops custom software, databases, and business intelligence solutions for companies throughout San Francisco, Silicon Valley, and the western United States.

Mark has served on the boards of numerous technical and community organizations, including the Professional Association for SQL Server, the Bay Area Association of Database Developers, and SofTECH. He leads the Bay Area Microsoft Database and Business Intelligence Community, and was selected by Microsoft as a Most Valuable Professional (MVP) for SQL Server. He and his family live in Marin County, just north of the Golden Gate Bridge.

TED: Why did you join Twitter?

MARK: To get the word out about professional group meetings I run, and to learn about what's happening in the Microsoft professional community.

TED: How long did it take you to do your first Tweet, and what was it?

MARK: My first Tweet took about one minute, to zero followers (my mother isn't on Twitter!!). I thought is was "Hello World," a common phrase for software developers, but the SocialBro app says it was "The San Francisco SQL Server User Group meets tomorrow at Microsoft. http://tinyurl.com/anlryx." This is one of the user groups I facilitate for software developers.

TED: What tips do you have for someone who doesn't know what to say on Twitter?

MARK: See what others are writing about and ReTweet! Also, check news sites and Tweet [shortened] links to their articles, with your comments. See what's happening in your profession and write about it.

TED: How many times do you Tweet per day or week?

MARK: I Tweet anywhere from one to ten times daily. It all depends on what's going on with my business and user groups. Sometimes I don't Tweet on the weekends if I'm not promoting a meeting or I don't read anything worth sharing. Sometimes I Tweet 40 plus times a day when I'm traveling to major events.

TED: What are your favorite Twitter tools?

MARK: HootSuite is my favorite Twitter tool and I couldn't live without it. I love being able to schedule Tweets rather than Tweeting real time, which is helpful for some of the informational Tweets I send. Also, TweetCaster, on my phone, for anytime access.

TED: How do you use Twitter for business? Do you use Twitter to research trends or your competitors?

MARK: I use Twitter to get the word out about my user group meetings and also to keep in touch with colleagues. Twitter is invaluable for keeping up with the international software community. . . . I love to check out the Twitter pages of companies that I admire and have great marketing departments. I also search on hashtags for topics I have particular interest in, like #sqlpass and #sqlserver, to see what the SQL software developers are talking about.

TED: What impact has Twitter had on your business?

MARK: Twitter has allowed me to reach the Bay Area software community to let them know about professional group meetings. Twitter has also made me well-known within the software and database community throughout the U.S. and abroad. Last year I was director of global chapters for the Professional Association for SQL Server (www.sqlpass.org), so I was in touch with user group leaders worldwide through Twitter. This resulted in many international followers and a whole lot of great friendships.

TED: What impact has Twitter had on your personal life, if any?

MARK: I stay loosely in touch with a certain group of personal friends via Twitter, often through Direct Messages. If something is urgent, however, I use text messaging. Most of my personal and professional communications are still via email because 140 characters simply aren't enough for most of my technical and business communications.

TED: What tips do you have for someone just getting started on Twitter?

MARK: First, set up your account and upload a photo, any photo or image. Then search for people or organizations you know and follow them to see how they are using Twitter. When you feel comfortable, start Tweeting at least three times a day. It takes a while to get your groove on, so don't give up if you don't think you're getting the hang of it.

TED: Who are your favorite people you follow?

MARK: @FredDavis, @MicrosoftBI, @AndrewBrust, @GFritchey, @MaryJoFoley, @BrunoAziza, @StrateSQL.

TED: Who are your favorite followers (people you met after they followed you)?

MARK: [When] I was director of global chapters for the Professional Association for SQL Server . . . that resulted in many international followers. Some of my favorites, though, are folks who ReTweet my Tweets, when they are of value to their followers. This really multiplies my reach. People who are frequent ReTweeters include @SQLServer, @SQLPASS, @JenStirrup, @AngelStreamline, and @retracement.

TED: What is your favorite Twitter story?

MARK: A couple of months ago I was on a flight to Dallas, and was online (thanks to @VirginAmerica and @gogoinflight). I received an email from a team member. He had just learned via Twitter that a major software company needed training in a new technology DesignMind is becoming well known for. After we compared notes, he responded via Twitter, and by the time I was back on the ground, we had exchanged emails with the client. We trained their local business intelligence team, and also their team in Bangalore, India!

TED: What else do you have to say about Twitter?

MARK: Twitter has allowed me to learn from, and communicate with, other software professionals around the world. It has been incredible in that sense. It can help spur a revolution or just help you find someone at a conference. If you have something important to say, your message can reach far beyond your network. It can be educational, fun, useful, or whatever you want it to be. It is all of those things wrapped into one easy-to-use tool.

CARRIE WILKERSON @CARRIEWILKERSON AND @BAREFOOT_EXEC

Carrie Wilkerson is an amazing woman. I don't remember exactly when and why I started following her on Twitter, but I'm so glad I did. Carrie Tweets many times a day and her Tweets are entertaining, thought-provoking, and educational. As you'll learn in this interview, she had to reverse-engineer her Tweets to understand why they are so popular and ReTweeted so often. She didn't intentionally create a Twitter strategy at first, but after she discovered she had over 15,000 followers without trying, she decided she'd better figure out why.

I do remember I was preparing a Twitter presentation a few years ago and noticed that Carrie was averaging over 4000 Tweets per month when I looked her up on TweetStats. The amazing fact is that she was doing all of these Tweets manually when she first started Tweeting. Today, she's created a strategy where she's Tweeting about 2,000 times a month with a combination of automated Tweets and live interactions.

Carrie is truly a Twitter success story, and I'm honored that she agreed to be interviewed for this book. I could have listened to Carrie and her stories for hours.

Business name: Barefoot Executive

Website/blog: http://barefootexecutive.tv

Joined Twitter: 2008

Followers: 120,116

Following: 94,202

Tweets: 68,099

Carrie Wilkerson is the voice of experience. From corporate life to teaching high school to direct sales, to information marketing and coaching, she has "been there and done that," professionally and personally. An "overnight mom" to two toddlers through adoption, her priorities instantly changed, and so did her workplace. She's now built several businesses and coached others to do the same while overcoming extreme debt, losing 110 pounds, and having two more children, for a total of four, aging from toddler to teen!

As "The Barefoot Executive," Carrie and her network of experts have quickly become the definitive resource for helping others achieve extra income and career goals while working from home. And, through BarefootExecutive.TV, she coaches clients to be their best selves no matter what their business model.

Currently Carrie is a mentor/coach/advisor to over 100,000 men and women as the Barefoot Executive through videos, podcasts, masterminding, mentoring, and live speaking. Not only a business expert but an expert *in* business, Carrie's work-at-home methods have inspired thousands and earned many awards, online and off.

A sought-after speaker, Carrie's mix of humor, real-life examples, and tough love translates to every audience, gender, genre, and generation.

Her passion is in teaching others to "Fill their stadium" with fans so that marketing is easy and business is abundant!

TED: I have been following you on Twitter for years, I think since you began.

CARRIE: Four years ago today.

TED: Happy Twitter Birthday!

CARRIE: I got a birthday note from Twitter today. I signed up in April, 2008, but I didn't really do anything until August, 2008.

TED: And that is what I find with most people I talk to about Twitter. They're afraid to Tweet because they don't know what to say.

CARRIE: Well, for me, I was just already so busy with business that I thought I didn't need one more place to be online. So I really was a late adapter, but then by October I think I had 15 or 16 thousand followers. I mean, it was nuts.

TED: Did you know that in January of 2009 you Tweeted over 4,000 times?

CARRIE: Yeah, so I got the hang of it. And now I probably Tweet way more than that, I would think—I don't know, I'll have to look.

TED: I don't know how accurate these stats are, but TweetStats says last month you did 2,826 Tweets.

CARRIE: That might be about right. That's about 100 a day, right?

TED: That's a lot of Tweets!

CARRIE: Yes, so after that first few months I remember I heard Scott Stratton of www. unmarketing.com speak at an event. He did a keynote at an event where we both spoke a few years ago. He was on Twitter for about a year and didn't see a lot of results. Then he decided to give it another try and just lived on Twitter for about 30 days. And then you gain significant momentum when you put some time in it like that and it changed everything. He just did a lot of Replies and ReTweets to get comfortable, then everything took off for him. I decided to take the same approach.

TED: I like what you wrote about pretending you're at a kid's birthday party and you are starting conversations with other parents around the fringe of the room.

CARRIE: Yep, people say I don't know what to talk about or I'm not that interesting. Well just talk about something. Talk about what they are talking about and just be relevant. And so many people try to *be interesting* and I think that's a mistake. I think instead, it's a very small change, but instead you *be interested* in other people. We have all been at that party whether it's a kid party or an adult party, where somebody walks in and tries to be interesting, tries to get us to look at them and converse with them. Then we have all seen the person that comes in and doesn't really add a lot but is pulling a lot out of other people, and is interested in other people. That's the person that people want to be around—because people want someone to show interest in them and not to show all the reasons why we should pay attention to somebody else. I think social media just follows those really basic tenets of human interaction. Don't be that guy or don't be that girl. Jonathan Mizel, who's an internet marketing expert, who has been around a long, long time, said to me once, "Some people demand attention and others command attention." And I think that if we come in and try to demand attention . . . that repels other people. But some people, by just who they are—magnetic and being interested in other people— they command attention without even meaning to. And if that's the case then social media is a really good fit, I think.

TED: Yes, that is so well said. That's so perfect. We have all been to those parties where people talk your ear off, and it comes off like *I don't care about you.*

CARRIE: Exactly, *I want to talk about me and less about you.* You know, I have an eight-year-old who wants to be on stage and on Broadway and I have no doubt she has the talent to do that, but she's really going through that phase of it all has to be about her. When we are in a group of people she really spends a lot of time trying to get the attention to her. So I am really [working] with her on [the concept that] if you spend time complimenting other people and drawing other people into the attention on them, the attention will naturally fall on you for being that person. When I walk into a room, people would say I'm charismatic or I'm magnetic or whatever. I don't work really hard at getting attention. The attention comes to me because I spend so much time focused on other people, and I think social media fits that, if you can use it for that, and that can be learned. It's not necessarily something you're born with, it can be learned. There are too many people trying to put the spotlight on themselves, when really the power comes in putting the spotlight on other people.

TED: There is so much of that on social media—so much self-promotion, it's all about me and I'm wonderful. I'm thinking, "No—you don't get it."

CARRIE: But they don't get it in real life, either. For people [who] ask "What are the rules about social media," it's the same rules that you have in real life, and so the people [who] don't get it in real life aren't going to translate it to social media, either.

TED: Yes, interacting on social media is no different from interacting with someone standing right in front of you.

CARRIE: Be kind and share, encourage others, and have manners.

People overcomplicate [Twitter]; it's just networking with technology. When I first started in business, I was about 100 pounds heavier than I am now and people don't ever believe that I've had a confidence problem. Well, when you deal with image issues your whole life, you don't want the spotlight on you, but . . . . I would go to these events with all these beautiful women—seriously, a high proportion of beautiful, thin, fit, have-it-all-together women—and then here comes me, 100 pounds heavier and dealing with infertility and depression and just not wanting any spotlight. And I remember, looking back now, I see I was one of the most popular people in the business. I was in the top 1 percent of achievers, I didn't have any trouble drawing people to me, and my team loved me. And looking back, if you reverse-engineered it, it's because I was so nervous about working the room and having attention on myself that I would literally stand outside the double doors at the ballroom and say, "There are people inside this room who are just as uncomfortable as me. There are people inside this room who are feeling inadequate and feeling inferior, I am going to find those people and encourage them and let them know we are in this together." So I would literally walk in the room and look for the people who were by themselves, the people who were looking at the floor, or people who were sitting alone, or the people who weren't talking or weren't bubbly and chatty like all the cliques were, and I would literally single out those people, spend time with those people and encourage those people. In doing so, I raised up an army of champions that loved me because of how I made them feel, when really it was self-preservation on how I was feeling. . .

I found even the people who seem like they have it all together—the beautiful people, the popular people—they are just as insecure as everybody else for the most part. And if you can go in and be the encourager, be the one asking them questions, making them feel important, then that's really how you gain power over the situation. And not that I did that intentionally, it really was self-preservation, but I can definitely see how that's what draws people to you. They want to be encouraged and need to be lifted up, they need to be included, they want to belong. And if you are the person who helps them feel that, then it's really a powerful thing.

I like to call that the Oz factor, leading back to Dorothy and the Wizard of Oz. When I first started in social media and all of a sudden I had thousands of people following me, I didn't know where they were coming from or who they were, what was getting all this attention. I kind of had this theory about the Wizard of Oz, and I said the Dorothy factor. They follow you because of the Dorothy factor. They want to follow somebody they think knows where they are going. They didn't expect Dorothy to have all the answers, right? They thought the wizard had all the answers. But Dorothy was willing to take them there. And Dorothy didn't insist on being in front of them, she wanted to walk beside them. So the Dorothy factor is somebody who knows where they are going and is happy for you to go along with them. And then the Lion factor is they want to follow somebody they think has courage, they don't care if you're scared. As a matter of fact, Dorothy showed her fear in several ways, but she kept going and she persevered. People like to know the person they are following has fears too, but is acting despite those fears. And the Tin Man factor, they want to follow somebody who has heart, not only somebody who has heart that loves you but loves what they're doing, and isn't afraid to care about things and causes and people. And so what I've found over the years is that people really love the fact that I am super emotional about orphans or care about people and what they are going through with their families. So there's the Tin Man factor, but then there is also the Scarecrow factor. They don't expect you to have all the answers, but they do want to know you're not afraid to use your brain.

So I always tease about the fact that I'm a blond, I'm a southern blond, but the fact is they like to follow people who aren't afraid to think things through, who aren't afraid to use their brains. It doesn't mean I have to be intellectual, it doesn't mean I have to be the smartest person in the room. But it does mean they like to see I am thinking about things and thinking through things and thinking along with them about things and not afraid to debate or discuss.

So that's a little bit of the Oz factor, but the other thing is in the Oz factor when they get to the Wizard they find out he's not the one with all the answers, but Dorothy helps him see they all had the answers within them all along, and I think that's true. No matter what your market, your service, your product, your business, I think that's true of the people following you—they tend to have the answers inside of them all along, and they really want to follow somebody who helps them on a process of self-discovery, or intelligent thinking, or loving or courage. And there are going to be flying monkeys, and witches, and poppies, and all kinds of obstacles along the way. But the fact is we weather those together. I think people don't necessarily want to be led by somebody in front of them, but somebody who is going to link arms with them on the Yellow Brick Road. That's kind of my whole leadership philosophy all in one. They are looking for a new model of leadership and it's not necessarily the guru-itis or this is what I think or this is how it has to be. But rather kind of Dorothy's approach to leadership.

TED: Now that you say all that, I see you do that every day on Twitter. I don't think you did it intentionally.

CARRIE: No, that's what I said. I totally reverse-engineered that. *Why are these people following me, what do they see?* You know, it's not something I do intentionally, it's really very organic, but I think it can be taught. I think people can do it intentionally if they choose, if they care enough to do that. But for me, I am uncomfortable with leaving people behind me. I really would rather it be all walking together and tripping up together. Of course, the only thing Dorothy and I are different about are the shoes. But it's just a matter of people being along for the journey with you, not necessarily you being the captain of the ship, so to speak. But yeah, that's very much how I lead.

And the other thing I think that's really important about social media and whether it's Twitter or Facebook, Pinterest or whatever, the best compliment I ever got and the comment I most often receive in person is, "You are just exactly like you are on Twitter, you look exactly the same, you sound exactly the same." There is no disconnect or disrupt, and I think that's so important. For instance, here's just an example, and I know you've probably been to an event where you've seen somebody and maybe they are 20 pounds heavier than their Twitter picture or 15 years older than their picture and there's an immediate disconnect, right? And so that disconnect, what's so powerful about that is that then I immediately mistrust everything else you have ever told me. *What else is she glossing over?* So if you're in business, there is an immediate retraction, we have to start over in our relationship because I am having some disconnect here.

I went to the drive-thru with my daughter yesterday at McDonald's after school. She really likes to go get smoothies, so we went through, and I am one of those moms. I am a McDonald's mom; sorry, everybody who isn't—don't send hate mail. Just kidding. Well, we were going through the drive-thru and a woman took my order. I live in a small town so I know most of the people who work at McDonald's, but a woman took my order, so I drive up to the window and it's this gigantic 6′ 5″ man who weighs about 350 lbs. taking my money. Well it took me a minute to recover. I was expecting the woman who took my order, right? And I immediately went, *Oh, wow, that's the disconnect we feel in social media when we are having engagement with somebody who is so friendly.* I could use some very high-profile industry names right here and say they're friendly, warm, bubbly, and very acceptable in social media but then you meet them in person and they are divas; their arms are linked, they are not accessible. There is a huge gap between who they are online and who they are in person. You have to take a minute to pause, and sometimes you never get that trust back. Sometimes you are so disillusioned that you start to question everybody else you meet in social media, too. So that's why I think a huge part of social media is, if you are not going to be there and engage personally or engage authentically, let people know that. So for instance, I have two Twitter IDs, Carrie Wilkerson is me, live and in person. I handle all of that myself. Barefoot_Exec is my old ID, the one I built under, primarily, but now it's just a feed. So it's my logo, and it says at the top, "This is the automatic content feed of Carrie Wilkerson the Barefoot Executive. For her live feed go to Carrie Wilkerson." So I am very upfront about the fact there is not going to be any engagement there, I am not following there, that is just content.

The mistake comes when people try to have their personal brand and use it as a content feed with no engagement. You have to be clear on what's what. People are pretty OK with the parameters if they just know what they are. I just wrote a big blog post about that this week, about *Dancing with the Stars* contestant Maria Menounos, how she is engaged with her followers and how that's going to make a difference in this competition for her. That she's not being a diva. And I think in business you have to pick your motive for social media, you have to know why you are there and then stick with it. So if you are there just to listen or just for customer service, that's fine. Make clear to your followers why you are on Twitter because if people try to engage with you and you don't engage back in a friendly way, then you are going to get a bad reputation. Whereas if they know why you are there and how you are going to be monitoring that, they are okay with it. Does that make sense?

TED: Completely. One of my pet peeves is people not having a clear strategy for Twitter and they not letting others know why they are on Twitter.

CARRIE: Yeah, and I think people are OK if you don't engage if they know you are not going to engage, right? So they don't expect Coca-Cola to engage. However . . . I have to say, if you are using case studies, Dr. Pepper is doing a really great job with social media, listening, interacting, ReTweeting, getting in the trenches, and continuing the conversation from their TV campaigns. They are doing a really nice job. So the small-business owner can do the same thing and you don't have to live there. There are a lot of social media purists who think it all has to be you and organic, and I disagree. I do my own personal Tweets, however, I do use things like Buffer App to schedule some Tweets through the day, and here's why: because I tend to go on little research binges where

I go, "Oh that's cool, I'm going to share that," or, "Oh, that's awesome!" So in a period of an hour I might have 15 things that I love and I want to share, but nobody can absorb all that. It's like sending information to a saturated sponge; it can't get it all at once. So I use Buffer App to kind of bookmark those things and trickle them out over the next few hours, so that they can get maximum viewing, sharing, etc. It also lets me measure my metrics and see who's clicking, who's ReTweeting, how popular, and what times my social media people are paying attention. I don't see anything inorganic about that, or inauthentic. I think if that were all I was doing, but I was pretending it was live, that's one thing. But my audience knows I am engaging and replying and I am there, so they don't mind so much that every once in a while there is something trickled out. You can use HootSuite or Social Own for some of those to schedule your Tweets if you want.

But again, if you are one of these marketers who's doing just that, and you are doing it every three hours even through the middle of the night when people know you're sleeping, that lacks authenticity and looks robotic. I think it's not as effective, unless you put a disclaimer on it and say, "Yep, I'm sleeping, this is automatically scheduled." I think [followers] tend to be a little more OK with that. I just use a variety of things.

Another thing I use is TwitterFeed; it's a free app that lets me share my friends' blogs automatically. So for instance, I have a list of people whose blogs I love and I usually read all my blogs at the same point every week or every day. If I were to share all of them as I am reading them, it would drown my followers. So as a courtesy to my followers I go to Twitter Feed. For instance, Bob Burg is one I always share. Just Kate is another one I always share as well as Michael Hiatt. I go into Twitter Feed and program in their information and then Twitter Feed automatically checks every 8 hours or 12 hours and if they have a new post it shares it with my audience. And so that's a way that I constantly have good content out there that I trust, but I am not jamming up the Twitter stream by sharing it all at one time. It helps me spread it out a little bit.

TED: Right, like sipping from a fire hose. We can easily overwhelm our followers with too much information.

CARRIE: And that is so much my personality: having a conversation and an interview. A resource share with me is really like trying to sip from a fire hydrant, it can be a little much. You probably get a little taste of that right now; it can be a little much, because that's how my brain works. But that allows me to kind of drip things out. I also use Tweet Old Posts, which is a plug-in for your

WordPress blog. It helps me recycle old blog posts of mine, and again you can set the parameters every 12 hours, every 24, every 36. That is how I keep some of my videos and blog posts in circulation. But I do label those as *From the Archives* or *Popular Post*, or something like that, just so people know that I am not pretending that's new content.

TED: Right, I hate it when it's Christmas Day and you are seeing people doing auto-blasts. Turn it off on the holidays, at least.

CARRIE: Yes, exactly, let's at least pretend that we are doing something organic here. So those are some of the things I use to help me stay current, but at the same time I am very present, too, I can pop in and out. That's what I love about Twitter. I can pop in and out on my phone while I'm standing in line at the grocery store. I can Tweet a picture while I'm experiencing something. So I can be present, but it doesn't have to be a time suck. But those other tools help me be present, seem more present than I actually am.

TED: Right, and you're a master at that, I have to say. Just be authentic, be you. You are trying to brand your business here and you are your business. Don't fool people.

CARRIE: Yeah, exactly. Either just be your business or just be you or just don't be. And if it overwhelms you, don't change all the rules midstream and just delete your account, and go away because you're not getting a big enough ROI. In my opinion, if you're not getting an ROI, you're not doing something right. Twitter has had a tremendous ROI for me.

TED: Yes, and analytics sounds like it's very important for you.

CARRIE: Yeah . . . on social media, I measure engagement. I can name ten high-level clients that I have gotten, and when I say "high-level" I mean like $25,000 contracts and more that I have gotten directly from my engagement in social media. I got my book deal because of Twitter. My publisher approached me on Twitter and said, "We have been following you for two years. We think you have a book in the making, would you write that for us?"

TED: You tell great stories on Twitter. Where do your stories come from?

CARRIE: Thanks, I do keep a little running dialogue about the Barefoot family. All my kids have nicknames like Baby Barefoot and Broadway Barefoot and then the Barefoot Junior and then the Barefoot Boy because he's the only son I have. And people like that, they like the human brand. Hasn't Gary V. been proof of that—people like for the brand to be humanized a bit? They love the little stories that I tell about my family or the stupid stuff I tell on myself, like, *Note to self—unbuckle the airplane seat before you try to get up*. Because everybody has done something like that, so they love that you are human.

TED: You are great at showing your vulnerabilities. That's what makes it so heartwarming to read your Tweets and blog posts.

CARRIE: Yes, I'm great at showcasing how stupid I really can be, and then I will say stuff all the time, that anybody can run a business, you don't have to be that intelligent to run a business, clearly. But yes, it's just we spend so much time in a world of celebrities who spend so much time air-brushing and covering up their flaws, I think that people really welcome the idea of somebody very flawed. And boy, wow, am I that! So, I don't mind talking about it.

The truth is, I don't share all my dirty laundry. I do believe there needs to be some level of privacy. Faith Popcorn is a trends predictor. I read an article by her a couple years ago that said the great thing about social media is arm's-length intimacy. I think I do that really well. My audience feels like they know everything about me, right? As a matter of fact, some people have boundary issues, really feel like we're buddies, that we're really, really close; they feel like they know everything about me. Except that I do have arm's-length intimacy, in that we are as close as I allow us to be. I am very careful. I rarely put my kids' names in social media. That's why they have nicknames. Everybody feels like they know my kids, they see their pictures. But they don't realize what they don't know. My husband's name is Mr. Barefoot; he's very rarely in social media. His picture is in very few places in social media, for privacy purposes. And they know how long we've been married, they know a little bit about our story. They know the romantic stuff he does, because being successfully married along with having a successful business is part of my brand. I want to help people see that that's possible. But yet I don't broadcast it when we have an argument. I think some people are too open and intimate in social media. People who are blogging about their divorces and blogging about the issues they're having—that's a little much, in my opinion.

So I think that arm's-length intimacy means you control the level of familiarity people have with you. Just as a result, people know that I battle with my weight all the time, so I'll be at a conference—literally this happened—I was at a conference and I was at the buffet table. I was just there as an attendee. I wasn't even there as a speaker, and I was at the dessert table and got this one small, little cookie. This woman next to me said, "Well, I thought you were on a diet, should you have that?" I went, "WOW, do I know you and why is that okay for you to say that?" So people are watching very closely and are paying very close attention.

We have a new term now, we say people are living "Vi-Carrie-ously" through me. But it's really true, that's why I think you have to be super careful. My parents' names and the town where they live, I am really careful with too many details. Because you do have to be smart, there are people with no boundaries, there are people with no scruples and there are people with blurred social lines. I know stories of people showing up at people's houses, and people calling their personal phone numbers. After nine years of having the same telephone number, I had to get an unlisted number, in a small town where I know everybody. It was really hard to do but we had some people who would look us up and call because we had connected in social media.

Those are extreme examples and I never felt scared and I never felt targeted or anything, but I do think you have to be a little careful about too much detail, so I would caution people that you can have some personal things. I do tell stories about my kids. I do tell things about my life but I am careful at the same time. So somebody who has been following me a long time, like you, you feel like you know a whole lot about my life, well, now you are going to step back and look a little different and say oh, okay, now I see what she's leaving out, now I see how careful she is with some of that. So that's part of it, too, and that's part of effective leadership. Seriously, if you are following Zig Ziglar or John Maxwell or Mary Kay Ash, any of the big names, and all of a sudden they are talking about marital troubles that they're having, yeah, a small part of their audience is going to relate to that and appreciate that, but a bigger part of the audience is going to say, "WOW, I wish I didn't know that."

TED: Right. I totally agree that some things shouldn't be shared with your audience.

CARRIE: Wow, that makes it hard for me to give credence to this other stuff.

TED: Too much information can be damaging to your reputation.

CARRIE: TMI. Yeah, you really have to be careful with TMI in my opinion.

TED: Yes. This is really great information and so much more than I expected. Thank you for sharing.

I love your story about how you turned around your life and everything. I did a similar thing for my wife and kids. I was working corporate jobs and I was never home. I had two young kids at home and I wanted to be part of their life so I quit my job and started consulting. I just walked away from a successful career of over 20 years and I was a consultant for 12 years. Now I am back in the workforce because of college tuition and the downturn in the economy. I love the stability of a corporate job but I miss my freedom.

CARRIE: I tell people it's not what you're walking away from. Quit worrying about what you walked away from and look at what you're walking toward. Look at all the benefits there. It's a big, huge difference.

TED: I know there are certain topics you stay away from like politics and religion because they polarize everybody. You can create a lot of controversy with just one Tweet.

CARRIE: Yes, I agree.

TED: Like Howard Shultz from Starbucks. He's going to stop donating to give any political contributions to anybody until things change.

CARRIE: Yep. All people have to do is look at what happened with the whole Susan G. Komen and Planned Parenthood thing, to see how social media can work against you. That was just a nightmare.

TED: That's great advice. So if somebody tries to engage you in politics, religion, or any controversial subjects on Twitter, do you ignore it or what do you say?

CARRIE: You know, it depends what the topic is. If they invite me to blog on parenting or if they ask my opinion, I will usually say something like, "You know I believe that parenting is fairly individualized based on the kid. I can tell you that I have four kids and I parent the four of them pretty differently." I have a kind of a nonanswer with some of that.

TED: OK. That makes sense. You let people know where you stand without revealing too much detail.

CARRIE: If it's a political thing, I will just out and out say, "I have learned that political issues are a lightning rod in social media and I avoid them."

TED: Thank you, Carrie, for sharing your story with us. You are a true small-business success story, and thank you for sharing.

ERIC JAN VAN PUTTEN @ERICJANVPUTTEN

I work with Eric Jan at Sitecore, where he is the marketing manager in our Netherlands office. I really enjoy working with Eric because he's a very creative marketer and loves to test new ways to get the word out about Sitecore. He got the job there by using social media, especially Twitter, to demonstrate his expertise. Today he continues to be one of our most creative marketers and he's a great resource for me when I want to bounce some ideas off another marketer. We always learn a lot from each other and we have a lot of fun working together. Eric does most of his Tweeting from our Sitecore corporate Twitter account, @sitecore_nl, so his personal Twitter stats don't make him look like a power Twitter user, but he is!

Business name: Sitecore (Netherlands)

Website/blog: www.marketingsteps.nl

Joined Twitter: Sometime in 2010

Followers: 641

Following: 404

Tweets: 2,129

Eric Jan Van Putten is the marketing manager at online marketing platform supplier Sitecore, Netherlands (www.sitecore.nl). He loves online marketing with its many facets, challenges, and possibilities. With a penchant for analyzing existing marketing channels, Eric Jan is always trying new ways and combinations to optimize their performance with a continuous focus on achieving ROI.

Eric Jan loves to keep up to date with technology and what it can mean for a person's life. He loves movies and TV series so he likes to search for new series and movies that he downloads (allowed in the Netherlands). He set up an automated system using CouchPotato and Sick Beard that scans automatically for new series episodes or movies that he puts on a wish list. When the system finds series or movies on his wish list, it automatically puts them on a file server, so his Apple TV 2 can play them.

Eric Jan also likes to read up on new marketing reports from analysts and experts like Forrester, Gartner, and HubSpot. Those are always great resources and full of ideas to try out later.

But all technology and marketing-related knowledge aside, he loves spending time on his sailboat. He loves sailing it on the edge, getting the most out of it while enjoying the elements.

TED: Why did you join Twitter?

ERIC JAN: I liked the idea that a simple platform leveled the playing field for organizations young and old, big and small. And that it is a great platform for personal branding is a nice extra.

TED: How long did it take you to do your first Tweet?

ERIC JAN: I don't exactly remember, but since then I have spent far longer on certain important tweets.

TED: Why did it take so long if you didn't Tweet right away?

ERIC JAN: I do remember that I needed a bit of time because it's the first step on a new channel. Although the follower list isn't very big (probably zero) you don't want to start with a stupid start.

TED: What was your first Tweet?

ERIC JAN: According to www.myfirsttweet.com it was *#durfttevragen: Iemand bekend met het Young Potential Programma van KPN*, which is, "Someone familiar with the KPN Young Potential Program" in English. Well, my first Tweet was to ask (dare to ask) if anybody knew the young potential program of a big enterprise called KPN. I was searching for a new job as I didn't like working for myself full time anymore. I wanted to search for a real opportunity within an organization that invests heavily in new potentials. I also wanted to work in an enterprise-level organization. I knew about the program from KPN and I asked if anybody knew somebody who could help me. The hashtag was of course the trigger to:

- Get the message out there

- Get an answer to my question (by the way, I never really did get an answer)

- Send out a message that would trigger people to follow me

TED: What tips do you have for someone who doesn't know what to say on Twitter?

ERIC JAN: I think it depends on how you would like to be perceived on Twitter (and online altogether). Would you like to be a clown? Start with a good joke. Would you like to just share what happens to you? Share that you just had a nice dinner (maybe with a bit.ly link to the recipe). Would you like to be the expert? Share short tips, links to your and other blogs.

TED: How many times do you Tweet per day or week?

ERIC JAN: I have two accounts: the @Sitecore_nl and my own @ericjanvputten. On the Sitecore account I try to post on the right times, about three to four times a day. For my own account I don't have a real target number. I would like to become an expert (with short personal break Tweets in between to give it a personal touch), so I Tweet when I have a tip or a blog I would like to share or did something within my expertise.

TED: What are your favorite Twitter tools (TweetDeck, HootSuite, Topsy, etc.)?

ERIC JAN: I try new tools every week or month; some stick; most do not. I tried HootSuite, Topsy, and Much, Much More Twitter, and other Twitter-related tools. But I like the following tools and I use them a lot:

- *TweetDeck v0.38.2.* I don't like the new versions as they removed a couple of very useful functions, for example the new followers column/functionally.

- *Crowdbooster.com.* I just use this to get notifications on which Tweets were most successful to try to repeat the same message. I also use this tool to easily see what the best time to Tweet is, and to track the growth of our follower base.

- *Bit.ly* (free version). Not 100 percent accurate, but it's integrated in TweetDeck so long URLs get shortened automatically and you can check online how your links are performing. I use the free version as the paid version is way too expensive, which is too bad because I would like to use the Sitecore shortened domain link also.

- *Sitecore Engagement Analytics.* All our activities, and also the Tweets with links, get tracking URLs from Sitecore Engagement Analytics. I could exactly see what Tweet, belonging to a bigger campaign or not, delivers what. This could be interested site browsers to demo requests and signups to webinars for example.

TED: How do you use Twitter for business?

ERIC JAN: I use Twitter for Sitecore in a couple of ways:

- *Generate Traffic.* With Twitter we can extend our branding online. We use Twitter to get more relevant followers, which we want to convert into known contacts in our systems. So we try to lead these followers to our website to get to know Sitecore better and to convert there on one of our assets.

  Offline we also use Twitter during tradeshows and events to let visitors know we are there. You can easily do this with the right hashtag. But a heads-up is in order; if you use the business account, don't overdo it with the Tweets, because most likely most of your followers aren't there and it can get annoying to them.

- *Engagement.* We "listen" for certain Sitecore keywords so if somebody asks a question we react on it. This can be a very straightforward question like @sitecore_nl or something like: "Does anybody have tips on #landingpages?"

We also share relevant content with our new followers based on their Tweets and bio's. This will also generate traffic, but the engagement value is much higher. This isn't an automated process, take your time and engage.

- ■ *Nurture.* What I really see is that social media, and thus also Twitter, is a great way to nurture your existing contacts. Send every now and then (roughly one in four) a commercial link to a free asset. Slowly nurture them till they are ready to be called/upsold or something else.

TED: Do you use Twitter to research trends or your competitors?

ERIC JAN: No, we don't monitor our competitors locally but they do monitor our competitors in the Sitecore Corporate Marketing department.

TED: What impact has Twitter had on your business?

ERIC JAN: We get business from our Tweets by promoting white papers and our local events. Twitter also helps us connect with our Sitecore community and build stronger relationships with our customers and prospects.

TED: What impact has Twitter had on your personal life, if any?

ERIC JAN: It got me this job!

TED: What tips do you have for someone just getting started on Twitter?

ERIC JAN: Personally, figure out what your role is and how you would like to be perceived. Next to that, figure out your goals and be consistent in your activities. Consistency is the key to success.

TED: Who are your favorite people you follow? Who are your favorite followers or people you met after they followed you?

ERIC JAN: I check my timeline on a regular basis, but I don't have a favorite person I follow. I'm not sure if I have any favorites. We have a lot of Sitecore Partners following us so they could be my favorites.

TED: What is your favorite Twitter story?

ERIC JAN: I have two favorite stories. Of course, my favorite story is that I landed this job by using Twitter. Almost two years ago, I saw the Tweet that Harry van Rossum sent out that he was searching for a marketing manager. I saw that Tweet and responded to it that I was going to take a look at the job vacancy.

The same day, I looked up Harry's profile on LinkedIn so he could see that I looked him up (getting into the back of his mind). I did that for a couple of days so I was sure he saw that I looked at his profile. After sending him my motivation letter and resume, I Tweeted to him that I had sent him an email in which I applied for the job. I've been working at Sitecore ever since!

Another favorite story is when I visited a Sitecore partner, the CEO showed me around his office. When I got to a certain department everybody stood up and already knew me by my Twitter accounts and Tweets before I got introduced to them. It was a very cool moment.

TED: What else do you have to say about Twitter?

ERIC JAN: Twitter is very effective and easy if you do the following:

- Figure out your goals
- Be consistent
- Work towards your goals
- If you are a marketer, measure everything
- Keep trying new tools

MICHELLE BUCHER @M_BUCHER

I "met" Michelle Bucher on Twitter a few months ago when I kept seeing her name pop up. Michelle learned quickly that following popular Tweeters and ReTweeting, Replying, and Mentioning their Tweets is a great way to get noticed. I started following Michelle because I liked what she was saying on Twitter.

I didn't know much about her but I saw she was quickly becoming a force on Twitter, and was impressed by how quickly she was becoming a Twitter power user so I wanted to learn more. It turns out Michelle has a very compelling, real Twitter success story.

Business name: MBucher Consulting

Website/blog: http://mbucherconsulting.com

Joined Twitter: 2011

Followers: 5,423

Following: 5,720

Tweets: 3,842

Michelle Bucher is a marketing consultant and social media marketer in Vancouver, British Columbia, with five years' experience in the marketing industry.

Michelle started her career in the marketing and communications department at the University of the Fraser Valley where she attended school for her bachelor's degree in business administration. After finishing university, Michelle started working full time as a marketing coordinator, while building her personal brand online. Michelle began blogging about marketing campaigns and establishing her brand presence via such social media platforms as Facebook, Twitter, and LinkedIn.

Her unique approach to personal branding led to a loyal following base and recognition of her marketing talents. After being laid off in 2010, Michelle was approached by a local business that had followed her on Twitter for some consulting work. This was soon followed by several other inquiries on Twitter about her services. Michelle recognized very quickly that she could establish a successful business using her social media presence with no advertising and next to no overhead.

Michelle's social media knowledge has become so well recognized that she has been approached to present at a social media conference in Vancouver.

Michelle's personal hobbies: aspiring extreme couponer, frequent road tripper, and lifelong learner of all things marketing.

TED: When did you get started on Twitter?

MICHELLE: I actually got started on Twitter about a year and a half ago now, in early 2011. I originally started using Twitter while I was working full time as a marketing coordinator. I wanted to kind of brand myself as a marketing expert and advance in my learning in what I was doing at work. I also wanted to showcase my skills to, I guess, the world. I knew that I wanted to move up into a higher-level position and having a social media presence and branding myself as a marketing expert. I knew that would be a huge benefit for me, versus not having a strong social media presence.

TED: How did you build your social media presence?

MICHELLE: I started getting into blogging about marketing campaigns, what I liked about them, what I didn't like about them. It kind of gave me a broader perspective on how people are doing marketing, especially the way I do it versus the way other people do it. I thought it would give me a better opportunity to learn. It was a really good thing for me. I think six months into that, I was actually laid off from my position, and that same day, I was actually approached by a company that asked me to do some consulting work for them. They had asked me to get into some marketing of their website and some social media for them. And I kind of just fell into the role of a marketing consultant. It actually worked really well for me, because shortly after that I had someone approach me on Twitter. He recently came across my profile and asked me to do some social media for his company. And it kind of just snowballed from there. I have had inquiries ever since about my work.

TED: So you were working full time as a marketing coordinator and learning social media as part of your job, you got laid off but then instantly got consulting jobs?

MICHELLE: It was about four hours into unemployment that I got my first, I guess, inquiry. This lady knew that I was a marketer and I guess she got to the point where she just needed someone to help her, so she contacted me. It worked out perfect.

TED: That's unbelievable. So, what tips do you have for somebody who doesn't know what to say on Twitter?

MICHELLE: You know, a lot of people say just to listen—that is definitely the first thing to do. I went on there looking for other like-minded people, marketing professionals, people talking about marketing and stuff. There are a lot of people sharing information out there so I essentially knew what my focus was. I wanted to learn more about marketing, specifically marketing campaigns, so I started following people—people similar to me, where I could learn from them—and kind of just watching and observing how people use Twitter, and reading a lot about it. There is obviously what they call the 'unwritten rules of Twitter' that you are just supposed to know but no one tells you. And a lot of it is just trial and error; you kind of just learn as you go.

TED: So whom do you learn from, who are the people you followed originally that you kind of figured out how to do it from watching them?

MICHELLE: There's obviously Chris Brogan, who's the main one that everyone seems to go to when they're learning social media or learning how to use social media effectively for businesses. Then there's always Mari Smith, a great social media thought leader. Hubspot.com has a lot of really good white papers that they send out to people. I find those very helpful. The higher-up people have been in social media since the beginning so I find them to be good to follow. They have essentially done what I've done, but years ago they started using social media. They have evolved into companies where they've been successfully training and consulting for well over five years now.

TED: Yeah, I notice the social media experts all listen a lot and they just kind of add value to conversation.

MICHELLE: Exactly, yes.

TED: Instead of just going out there and blasting away like some of these people do.

MICHELLE: You will also find that a lot of people are out there just to do self-promotions and discounts and shout, "Buy my product!" They will have a lot of people unfollow them, because you don't want to be advertised or sold to every minute of the day. It gets to be a bit much for people at times.

TED: Yes, it's overwhelming. How many times a day do you Tweet?

MICHELLE: I usually Tweet every two hours. I actually find that I get the most click-through while I'm sleeping so I use HootSuite to schedule Tweets. HootSuite is probably my favorite program I use and I usually will schedule my Tweets a couple days in advance. I let it automatically run for me while I'm at work or doing something else for a client or on a jobsite, those kinds of things, so at least I always have a consistent presence for my followers. They are always seeing something from me, whether it's live or scheduled.

TED: So what kind of Tweets do you schedule as opposed to the Tweets you do live?

MICHELLE: I actually have taken a different approach to my social media instead of promoting myself as a social media expert. I blog a lot about marketing campaigns, commercials, anything I find of interest in the field of marketing and then I just promote my blog through my Tweets. So I branded myself as more of like a communication hub or a place where people can find information. I have found it's been very helpful for me because people click on my links, go read my blog, and notice that I'm a social media marketing consultant. It seems that is how I get all my inquiries.

TED: So you just write blog posts and then you schedule Tweets that link to the blog posts throughout the day and night?

MICHELLE: Yes, and people respond to me. People ReTweet my blogs and then when I have some free time, I thank them for the ReTweets and follow them back. It's hard to be on Twitter 24 hours a day, so this approach works well.

It's nice to be able to break up my live Tweets. From a blog post to another blog post, you are creating communication with other people as opposed to just always promoting yourself. It's a good thing to do.

TED: That's one thing I noticed you do very well. You thank people for ReTweeting your Tweets, and you thank people for following. Some people do that for a while, but I don't see people do it as consistently as you do.

MICHELLE: I like when people do it for me and I know it's one of those things they say is an "unwritten rule of Twitter."

TED: Yes, it builds that relationship with people. People like to be acknowledged, especially publicly online.

MICHELLE: Yeah, and it shows that it's not just a 100-percent-you kind of thing, that you are there to create communication with people and interact with other people. And I appreciate when people ReTweet my stuff, especially when they have a large following base. So it's really nice to just thank them for the ReTweets. It doesn't take very long to do, so it's definitely something I would recommend that people do.

TED: Do you do that a couple times a day or once a week? How often do you thank people?

MICHELLE: It really depends, because I manage a bunch of different social media accounts for people. I usually go into my social media while I'm doing it for other people and I do that daily. There will be times where I will sit down around 11:00 and I will start going through all my social media accounts. And then sometimes around 4:00 in the afternoon I will do it again. There are sometimes when I will have to go to a jobsite so I do it at like 6:00/7:00 in the morning. It kind of varies because my schedule varies as well.

TED: How do you decide if you will follow someone?

MICHELLE: I find the more and more you're on Twitter, the more you can read someone's profile very easily. I find if I go into someone's profile and it's all about them, like they are just promoting themselves, you kind of know whether someone is going to follow you back. You also know that if you do follow them, it is all just going to be about them.

TED: There's nothing worse than following someone who constantly self-promotes and adds no value to Twitter conversations. I try not to follow people like that. I always look at their Twitter page to see what they've Tweeted in the past. So say I hired you as a consultant, how would that look, how would we work together?

MICHELLE: It depends on what you're looking for, if it's a marketing consultant or social media marketer, or just like overall business planning—those kind of things.

TED: Yes, so say, as a social media consultant.

MICHELLE: OK. I usually do, obviously, a first interview with people looking to see what it is they are looking for. People's perception about social media and how it works for business are very, very different. There are some people who understand it does take time. It takes communication and finding the right following, like segmenting your Twitter followers. Then there are other people who just kind of assume because I'm managing their social media, their sales should increase. So it's just a matter of sitting down, educating them, and looking to see what they want to get out of social media. Once I understand their objectives, I can draw up a really good social media action plan that will suit their needs. I have people in various industries, from restaurants, which will be a male and female audience, and then I have female clothing stores in the West End, and a female gym, so I have to specifically target certain people. It's always good to know your target audience beforehand.

TED: Tell me about this, you said you segment the users. What do you mean by segmenting the users?

MICHELLE: It depends. Like I said, I have a gym that's a female-only gym, so of course, if I want to increase their following base, I find females. You can't just follow males and you can't just follow random companies because you don't know if there are females in those companies. So you essentially want to find the right target audience that may be interested in the gym. You Tweet health or exercise tips, so you can find the right people who may want to join the gym.

TED: So how do you find new things to Tweet about?

MICHELLE: I just watch and observe a lot of things. I like to find the Twitter Trends that are going on in and around my area or the area where my clients are based, and then play up on those. I find Twitter Trends are very helpful.

TED: So you look at the local trending topics on Twitter?

MICHELLE: Yeah, and actually here's a perfect example for you. In November I wrote a blog post about Starbucks because they were just about to launch their new light-roast coffee. They are trying to target the people who are drinking McDonald's coffee, because it's a lighter roast than Starbucks. So I wrote a blog post about the new Starbucks campaign, and I don't want to say it went stale, but I promoted it for a while, a few people read it and I left it alone. Then in January I noticed that Starbucks light-roast was actually trending on Twitter and I used that opportunity to promote my blog because it was one of the top-trending topics in my area. So it actually worked very well: I got quite the click-through because of it being a trending topic. People want to see what's trending and what people are talking about in their area. If someone is interested in Starbucks and they see it's a trending topic, my blog becomes perfect content for them.

TED: So one thing you could do is see what's trending in your area on Twitter, write a blog post related to it, and then Tweet about it?

MICHELLE: Of course, that is actually how I got started. I think one of my first blog posts was about Fruity-Pebbles. I actually didn't understand why it was trending on Twitter, but it was one of the top trending topics. It ended up being a wrestler, I believe, was threatening another wrestler. He was telling him he was going to feed him Fruity-Pebbles because he was weak. I wrote a blog post about that and got quite a few clicks because people were wondering why Fruity-Pebbles was trending on Twitter. That ended up driving them to my blog.

TED: So the Twitter Trends tells you what exactly to Tweet about and what to write about?

MICHELLE: Yes, if people are looking for inspiration, those are really good things sometimes to follow.

TED: Yeah. Tell me about some Twitter disasters you've heard about.

MICHELLE: I actually wrote a blog at the end of the year, it's probably my favorite blog and it's actually the top ten social media slip-ups of 2011. I personally haven't seen any with my clients, not yet at least, but I have read about certain ones. A major car manufacturer outsourced their social media to a social media company and the person who was managing their account was getting upset with the traffic around the area that he was in. He used the F word on their corporate Twitter account by mistake, and even though it was deleted within a couple hours, enough people saw it. That didn't look very well for Chevrolet, and I would assume that the social media company actually lost that account because of that mistake.

A couple weeks ago I was on Twitter and noticed Rogers Communication had actually paid for a Sponsored Tweet to sit on the top of the page all day. They were trying to get a viral promotion going. I guess people saw the Sponsored

Tweet with a specific hashtag and were starting to complain about Rogers. People were Tweeting about how terrible their service was, how mad they were because Rogers increased their prices, and how bad the customer service was. The worst part was that people were adding the special promotional hashtag to their complaints. So people essentially spent the day complaining about Rogers Communication and promoting their competitors. It wasn't what Rogers was looking for when they started their social media campaign, and it was amazing to see how much backlash they got about it. The negative publicity was so bad that it was actually picked up by a couple of newspaper outlets. It was quite the story going around the internet about how much negative PR they were receiving from their social media. The other news outlets started writing about it as well.

TED: So word travels fast on Twitter.

MICHELLE: It does, and a lot of people were saying if they had decent customer service to begin with, they wouldn't have this problem.

TED: Right. I can't believe a company can provide a product or service and not provide excellent customer service these days.

MICHELLE: So I guess they have to review their customer service before they go into the next social media strategy they do.

TED: So another lesson a business could learn is you can't ignore Twitter because people are talking about you on there anyway.

MICHELLE: Of course, and it's the best way for people to be able to communicate with companies directly.

TED: Go where they are talking about you and reach out.

MICHELLE: And of course, I know Go Daddy had an issue as well during the Super Bowl; they have very risky campaigns. When Go Daddy was having a lot of issues or people were complaining about them, we were actually searching out people who were complaining about them, whether they were mentioned in there, like with the ad-find or whether they were hashtagged or just mentioned, but they were actually responding back to each and every one of them. So either we were working on our commercials or thank you for your feedback or looking into it—they were actually good at being proactive and getting back to people, which is really good to see.

TED: What else do you want to say about Twitter? I know it's really changed your life.

MICHELLE: It really has. I am actually quite amazed with how it has changed. I wanted to get into consulting for a while, but I knew the normal path that most people take, they work in a marketing position for 10, 20 years and then get into doing consulting. Again, I've done consulting for people, just one-off jobs while I was working full time, and it seemed to just fall into place perfectly for me. Like I said, my first lady messaged me on Facebook and was asking for help. The second client I ever got actually messaged me on Twitter, same with the third, the fourth, and the fifth; and it kind of just snowballed from there. I seem to get inquiries all the time on Twitter for my services. I actually had a lady from New Jersey this morning message me on Twitter asking about pricing, so it's been great and I actually will be presenting at a conference about Twitter this summer.

TED: So you have no formal training in social media or Twitter; you have just done it and observed others. Do you think others can be as successful as you without formal training?

MICHELLE: Yes, and you know there is not much formal training that you can get to be successful at Twitter. I know certain universities around here offer social media training, but you really don't learn it unless you're on there and you observe and you see what works and what doesn't, and who to follow and how to follow them, and why you should. You can write a blog post or a Tweet on Twitter that doesn't get a lot of click-through, and you change a little bit of the wording and you know, you get a couple hundred clicks just because of the way the words have been changed.

TED: I've heard it's like writing headlines or subject lines for emails. You want to catch their attention and get their interest.

MICHELLE: Yeah, give them a reason to click, especially if you start having a larger following. Your Tweet lasts maybe 15 seconds and then it's gone.

TED: You mentioned the unwritten rules of Twitter. Tell me more about them.

MICHELLE: Obviously you are supposed to thank people for following you in appreciation, and then, of course, the ReTweets, but I think the big one that a lot of people don't know about is the Twitter following limit because it's not published anywhere. I have only learned about this doing social media accounts for other people, and especially my own, how you can follow up to 2000 people, then you kind of hit that wall and you can't follow anymore until you have a certain amount following you back. And then of course once you get there—

they essentially only let you increase by about 200 or 300 more followers than you have yourself, and a lot of people don't even know that that following limit exists until you actually hit that limit yourself.

TED: So that explains why I see some people with 20,000 people they are following and they have 20,000 followers.

MICHELLE: Yeah, or you'll find—and again this comes back to where you can really read someone's Twitter account—someone's following you and they have 2,001 people that they're following and they only have a couple hundred followers, they've either just started their Twitter account or they are just looking for followers and they've hit their max, so they really can't go anywhere else until they get about 1820 followers themselves.

TED: How do you feel about people who automatically follow you back who send you an automated message?

MICHELLE: To be honest with you, I don't read any of the direct messages, because they are all "Thanks for the follow-up, please join me on Facebook" and a lot of them are, "I have a free gift for you." I like free stuff, it's fun, but when you get 15 to 20 of those a day it becomes a bit much, and I have had people direct message me who I don't see for weeks and weeks because I don't go into my direct message, because it's all just spam, essentially. I would actually like to be able to opt-out of the direct message option if I could.

TED: I have heard that from a lot of people. I hope Twitter adds that option in the future.

MICHELLE: I was just dealing with a client earlier today who is on Facebook but not on Twitter and they don't see the value in being on Twitter, because to them it's just Facebook status updates. But I find that you're able to segment your followers a lot better than you are on Facebook, and when I search that [client's name] on Twitter, they have a ton of people talking about them. Lots of people talking about how much they love their product, other people are talking about they are in the physical location. Other people just talking about the store in general, how much they really like it. So they have a lot of positive PR out there and lots of people talking about them, but they don't have a presence on there themselves. So I find that kind of interesting.

TED: Yes, that's interesting. Do you think you can convince them that they need to establish a presence?

MICHELLE: Yes, I am going to work with a company on that and change their mind.

TED: Good, perfect. OK, well, thank you very much for this interview, Michelle. This is such a great story and thank you for sharing.

CONCLUSION

As you see, Twitter can be a very powerful marketing tool for your business. All of these people have embraced Twitter, which has helped grow their businesses and build a strong online following.

In the next chapter, I'll introduce you to some very skillful Twitter power users who are considered to be the "best of the best."

Power Twitter Users

Of course this book wouldn't be complete if I didn't share a list of who I consider power Twitter users. These are the people I consider the most influential Twitter users for one reason or another. Some of these people are influential by the sheer number of followers they have, while others are influential because of the innovative ways they use Twitter.

Here's a list of some of the people I follow and consider my Twitter mentors. I study how they use Twitter to see what works for them and use their best practices in my Twitter strategy. Of course I follow a lot more people, but these are the Twitter users who teach me the most about using Twitter effectively.

I highly recommend you create a list of people in your niche who use Twitter well. Every niche has its own power users or thought leaders. Follow them and study how they use Twitter. Learn from them and use their best practices in your Twitter strategy. Don't reinvent the wheel. Watch what they do and do the same.

@CHRISBROGAN

Chris Brogan is a social media thought leader and one of the most influential social media users online today. Chris is the president of Human

Business Works, helping companies with customer acquisition and community nurturing by amplifying the human digital channel. Chris has worked with companies like Citrix Online, Ford, Microsoft, PepsiCo, AMD, Sony Electronics, GM, Cisco, and many more.

He is also the author of many bestselling books, including *Social Media 101: Tactics and Tips to Develop Your Business Online, Trust Agents and Google+ for Business: How Google's Social Network Changes Everything*.

Chris Tweets frequently and is constantly engaging others in lively conversations on Twitter. He's a master at "listening" on Twitter to find interesting conversations as well as helping others with ReTweets and Mentions.

@JEREMIAHOWYANG

Jeremiah Owyang became one of the first social media celebrities while he was an analyst at Forrester Research. By blogging and Tweeting frequently, Jeremiah became one of the most recognized thought leaders in the social media space. He eventually left Forrester Research to start the Altimeter Group with Charlene Li, who is another social media thought leader. Today Jeremiah is a frequent keynote speaker and the author of many industry research reports.

@CHARLENELI

Charlene Li also worked at Forrester Research before leaving to start the Altimeter Group. Charlene is a recognized social media expert, keynote speaker, and the author of many recognized research results. Charlene became famous on the social media scene in 2008 when she wrote *Groundswell* with Josh Bernoff, which was voted one of the best business books in 2008. Charlene was named one of the 100 most creative people in business by *Fast Company* in 2010 and one of the most influential women in technology in 2009. Charlene is a frequently quoted expert and has appeared on *60 Minutes*, *The PBS News Hour*, *ABC News*, and *CNN*. She is also frequently quoted by *The Wall Street Journal*, *The New York Times*, *The Economist*, *Businessweek*, *USA Today*, *Reuters*, and *The Associated Press*.

@BRIANSOLIS

Brian Solis is another social media guru who has studied and influenced the effects of social media and disruptive technology on business, marketing, entertainment, and culture. Brian works with enterprise organizations to research market trends, disruptive technology, and emerging business opportunities. He also works with executive management and social media leadership to develop new strategies and align teams around initiatives that enable business objectives and priorities.

Brian recently joined the Altimeter Group as a principal and a well sought-after keynote speaker and best-selling author. Brian's books include *Engage* and *The End of Business as Usual*.

@GUYKAWASAKI

Guy Kawasaki is the co-founder of Alltop.com, an "online magazine rack" of popular topics on the web, and a founding partner at Garage Technology Ventures. Previously, he was the chief evangelist of Apple. Kawasaki is the author of ten books, including *Enchantment, Reality Check, The Art of the Start, Rules for Revolutionaries, How to Drive Your Competition Crazy, Selling the Dream,* and *The Macintosh Way*.

Guy does a lot of his Tweeting personally, which is complimented by some automated Tweets and Tweets from his social media team. He's great at sharing valuable industry information as well as having fun on Twitter.

@GARYVEE

Gary Vaynerchuk is a *New York Times* and *Wall Street Journal* bestselling author who is also a self-trained wine and social media expert. Gary became famous when he began video blogging in 2005. He has close to a million followers on Twitter and was included in *BusinessWeek's* list of the top 20 people every entrepreneur should follow. Gary's first business book, *Crush It! Why Now Is the Time to Cash in on Your Passion,* hit *The New York Times, The Wall Street Journal* and the Associated Press bestsellers lists in its first weeks of publication in 2009. It maps out Gary's road rules for how to "crush it" in today's business market by following your passion and building your own personal brand. His second *New York Times* bestseller—published less than two years after *Crush It!—The Thank You Economy* (March 2011), details the effect of social media on business and has become required reading for business leaders. In spring 2009, Gary and his brother A.J. launched VaynerMedia, a new breed of agency that helps Fortune 500 companies like Campbell Soup Company, PepsiCo, Green Mountain Coffee, the NY Jets, the NHL, and the NJ Nets find their social media voices and build their digital brands.

@PETERSHANKMAN

Peter Shankman became a recognized social media expert when he started Help a Reporter Out (HARO) in 2008. HARO is a service that was designed to help reporters find subject-matter experts for their news stories. Since 2008, HARO has published more than 75,000 journalist queries, has facilitated nearly 7,500,000 media pitches, and has marketed and promoted close to 1,500 brands to the media, small businesses, and consumers. In addition to HARO, Peter is the founder and CEO of The Geek Factory Inc., a boutique marketing and PR strategy firm located in New York City, with clients worldwide. Peter is also a popular keynote speaker, author, and is a frequent subject-matter expert on news broadcasts.

@APLUSK

Ashton Kutcher became a social media icon when he declared he was going to be the first Twitter user with a million followers and challenged CNN to beat him. This was a very bold statement at the time because most people on Twitter only had a few hundred followers and celebrities only had a few thousand. The challenge generated tons of publicity for Twitter and showed the power of social media. Kutcher did beat CNN to the one-million-followers mark, raising over $100,000 for charity in the process.

I don't usually follow many celebrities, but I do follow @APlusK because he uses Twitter extremely well to generate a buzz and let his feelings be known.

@LADYGAGA

Lady Gaga? Yes, I started following @LadyGaga after she crossed the 20 million follower mark. I figured anyone with over 20 million followers is doing something right. I was pleasantly surprised when I saw @ladygaga does Tweet frequently and engages in real conversations with her followers. She's built a huge fan base with her music and her Twitter activity solidifies an already strong relationship. Whether you are a Lady Gaga fan or not, I highly recommend following her to see the real power of Twitter when it comes to relationship building. I also follow her to see how she generates over $30 million per year by doing endorsed Tweets. She's very subtle with her endorsed Tweets, which is an art form in itself.

BUILD YOUR OWN POWER TWITTER LIST

It's your turn to build your own Power Twitter list. Who are the most influential people in your industry? Do a Twitter Search and see if they are active on Twitter. See if they are active on other social media platforms like LinkedIn, Facebook, or on their own blog. See how they use Twitter and social media to build the brand and relationships. Incorporate their best practices into your social media strategy and you will see a dramatic improvement in your social media presence.

Chapter 11

What's Next?

At first glance, Twitter looks incredibly simple and doesn't look useful to most people. Once you get under the hood, you see how powerful Twitter really is. Twitter is proof that marketing doesn't have to be complicated. With Twitter, you can send short but effective messages that spread the word about your brand to more people faster than ever imagined. Twitter is currently growing at a faster rate than sites like Facebook and LinkedIn, and shows no signs of slowing down.

What's next? That's completely up to you. The fact that you've read this far into this book tells me you understand Twitter can be a powerful marketing tool, when used properly, and you want to learn how to use it effectively. After reading this book, you now know more about Twitter than most small-business owners and most Twitter members. What have you learned?

- You know the fundamentals of Twitter, including the Twitter lingo.
- You know how to use Twitter Search.
- You know how to set up your profile so you will be found on Twitter and Google searches.
- You know how to create an effective Twitter strategy for your company.

- You know how to build a strong, powerful network of Twitter followers.
- You know how to find like-minded people to follow and collaborate with.
- You know how to use Twitter Tools to enhance your Twitter experience.
- You know Advanced Twitter techniques such as using Twitter Lists, lead generation, brand building, creating viral Tweets, and creating successful Twitter contests.
- And so much more.

Don't stop now. If you are just getting started on Twitter, complete your profile including uploading a custom, branded Twitter background. Start following the leaders in your industry and "listen" to what they're saying. Start Tweeting links to your blog posts. Start engaging with other Twitter users. Start slowly until you gain confidence, then get out there and use what I taught you in this book.

If you've been using Twitter for a while, create or update your company Twitter strategy based on you learned in this book. Create a Twitter contest. Make a goal to double the number of people who follow you. Spend more time supporting your followers by ReTweeting, Favoriting their Tweets, and Mentioning them. Start using the Twitter Tools I mentioned to enhance your Twitter use and so you can measure your Twitter success.

Twitter is one of the hottest social media sites on the internet today. Ride the Twitter wave while it's peaking and you will be recognized as a leader in your industry. Twitter is one of the easiest tools to use to spread the word about you and your company, so take advantage of this powerful, free tool.

By the time this book is published, there will be many new advancements in Twitter and social media. I invite you to visit www.tedprodromou.com/twitter frequently, where I will be posting the latest and greatest Twitter developments.

Don't be overwhelmed by the infinite possibilities presented by Twitter. Pick one thing you learned in this book and master it. Keep mastering one Twitter technique at a time, and I'm sure you will see dramatic results virtually instantly.

To your Twitter success!

About the Author

Ted Prodromou is an Online Marketing/SEO Analyst for Sitecore, specializing in search engine optimization, pay-per-click campaign management and social media marketing. Ted has been working on the internet since 1991, when commands like AWK and GREP helped you navigate the internet before the browser was invented.

In his past life, Ted worked for high tech companies IBM, DEC and Cellular One before starting his own consulting firm in 1999. Ted lives in Marin County, California with his wife Ellen, his daughter Alicia and son Mike.

Ted is also the author of *Ultimate Guide to LinkedIn for Business*, Entrepreneur Press 2012. You can learn more about Ted at www.tedprodromou.com.

Index